The Naxalite Movement in India

The Naxalite Movement in India

PRAKASH SINGH

Rupa & Co

Copyright © Prakash Singh 1995

An Original Rupa Publication

First published 1995
Second impression 1999

Published by
Rupa & Co
7/16, Ansari Road, Daryaganj, New Delhi 110 002
15 Bankim Chatterjee Street, Calcutta 700 073
135 South Malaka, Allahabad 211 001
P. G. Solanki Path, Lamington Road, Bombay 400 007

Cover illustration: Supriya S. Lamba

Typeset in 11/13 pt Palatino by
Print Line
S-343, Greater Kailash II
New Delhi 110048

Printed in India by
Gopsons Papers Ltd
A-14 Sector 60
Noida 201 301

Rs 195

ISBN 81-7167-294-9

श्रीभगवानुवाच--
कालोऽस्मि लोकक्षयकृत् प्रवृद्धो लोकान् समाहर्तु-मिह प्रवृत्तः।
ऋतेऽपि त्वां न भविष्यन्ति सर्वे येऽवस्थिताः प्रत्यनीकेषु योधाः
तस्मात् त्वमुत्तिष्ठ यशो लभस्व
जित्वा शत्रून् भुङ्क्ष्व राज्यं समृद्धम्।
मयैवैते निहताः पूर्वमेव निमित्त-मात्रं भव सव्यसाचिन्।।

Lord Krishna said:

I am the terrible Time, the destroyer of people, and am here proceeding to destroy them; even without you, all these warriors in every division shall cease to be.

Therefore arise and attain fame, and conquering your enemies, enjoy a flourishing kingdom. By Me alone have these been killed already. O Savyasāchin (Arjuna), you be merely an instrument.

(Bhagavad Gita, XI, 32-33)

CONTENTS

Preface

1. **The Spark**—Stirrings In Naxalbari   1

2. **The Flame**
   2.1 A New Party Is Born   15
   2.2 Ideas That Ignited   25

3. **The Fire**
   3.1 Andhra Pradesh—Srikakulam   37
   3.2 West Bengal—Midnapur And Birbhum   47
   3.3 Bihar And Uttar Pradesh   54
   3.4 Other States   61

4. **The Blaze**   67

5. **The Flicker**
   5.1 Cracks In The Party   81
   5.2 Post-Mazumdar Period   94

6. **The Embers**
   6.1 People's War Group—Andhra, Madhya Pradesh
   And Maharashtra   105
   6.2 The 'New Left' In Bihar   120
   6.3 Profile Of Violence   131

7. **Retrospect And Prospect**   137

Appendices
   A Spring Thunder Breaks Over India   165
   B Biographical Sketches   170
   C 'Open Letter' From Kanu Sanyal And Others   178
   D Number And Percentage Of Population Below Poverty
   Line By States, 1972-73   182
   E Number And Percentage Of Population Below Poverty
   Line By States, 1987-88   183

References   184
Select Bibliography   190
Glossary   194
Index   195

PREFACE

The Naxalite movement erupted violently in 1967, its flames spreading to almost all parts of the country. Some of the finest brains and the cream of India's youth in certain areas left their homes and colleges to chase the dream of a new world, a new social order. Two decades had passed since the dawn of Independence and yet large segments of the Indian population—peasants, workers and tribals—continued to suffer the worst forms of exploitation. The peaceful political process, it was felt, would not be able to bring about the necessary change because vested interests controlled the levers of power, regulated the wheels of industry and had a feudal stranglehold over the predominantly agrarian economy. An armed struggle was the only way out, they thought.

It was in such an environment that there was a spark in a small village, Naxalbari, on the tri-junction of India, Nepal and what is today Bangladesh, and the "prairie fire" spread within a few years to distant parts of the country. There were uprisings of peasants and tribals and also urban actions marked by acts of terrorism. The movement came to be compared with the Huks of Philippines, the Al Fatah of Palestine and the Tupamaros of Uruguay. Some even dreamt of liberated zones turning to little Vietnams. These dreams were to be shattered. Intra-party differences and the counter-insurgency measures of the government led to gradual disintegration of the movement.

The flame was doused, but the embers remained—and there was a resurgence of the Naxalite movement in a virulent form in Andhra Pradesh and Bihar in the eighties. The People's War Group, with a firm base in the Telengana area, spread its tentacles to the adjoining areas of Madhya Pradesh, Maharashtra and Orissa. In Bihar, the administrative paralysis, economic bankruptcy and exacerbating social tensions are building up a frightening scenario, and in that welter of disorder the Naxalite violence is rising steeply, particularly in the south-central districts of the state. In all, ten states of the Union are affected.

The Naxalite movement has ebbed and flowed during the last more than a quarter century of its existence. Naxalism arose from certain basic factors—social injustice, economic inequality and the failure of the system to redress the grievances of large sections of people who suffered—and continue to suffer—as a result therefrom. These factors unfortunately continue to exist, perhaps in a more aggravated form. The embers would therefore continue to simmer; occasionally there might even be a violent flame or a raging fire depending on the volume of popular resentment and the presence of a master-brain to orchestrate those into a well coordinated movement.

The idea of writing this book germinated in my mind as far back as 1972 while I was serving in the Ministry of Home Affairs. My assignments had given me the opportunity to see the movement from close quarter and even interact with some of its top leaders including Charu Mazumdar himself. I felt that the movement represented a sincere, even if misguided, attempt to change a system which according to large sections of the people was not working in a fair and just manner. The writing work however could not be pursued, mainly because I moved from one high pressure job to another, serving in different trouble spots of the country. Nevertheless I took the care to keep myself abreast of the developments on the subject and, during my tours to different areas, kept on collecting whatever material I could lay my hands on. I also felt that I would be able to do justice to the subject only after I was free from the constraints of service. And so, after superannuation, I picked up the threads, and the end-product is placed before the readers.

Naxalism is a much abused term. The authorities playing second fiddle to vested interests in an area use this terminology to brand anyone crying for social or economic justice and justify repressive measures against him. Some Naxalite groups which have been indulging in senseless violence are also to blame for the misconception. Basically however, shorn of polemics, it represents the struggle of the exploited peasant, the deprived tribal and the urban proletariat for a place in the sun, for social and economic survival. The system has to provide this minimum. If it does not or cannot, the consequences are bound to be disastrous. Jaya Prakash Narayan, while touring the Naxalite affected areas of Bhojpur (Bihar) on June 12-13, 1975, exhorted the people to shun the path of violence and work for 'total revolution.'

Addressing the crowd at Narayanpur, he said: "If in five years from now nothing changes, I will not ask you to give up Naxalism." One wonders what he would have said today.

I would like to place on record my deep sense of gratitude to all those who helped me in the preparation of the book. Prof S.D. Tendulkar of the Delhi School of Economics and Ms Jayati Ghosh of the Jawaharlal Nehru University helped me in understanding the nuances of Indian economy. Ms Seema Alavi of the Jawaharlal Nehru University enabled me to get in touch with the right persons on different subjects. Shri Keki Daruwalla and Shri Arvind N. Das took the trouble of going through some chapters and offered valuable comments. I am particularly grateful to Shri Asish Kumar Roy for permitting me to reprint the biographical sketches from his book *The Spring Thunder and After*. Sri N.R. Banerji and Sri Nehchal Sandhu were good enough to collect volumes of published material on the subject and make the same available to me. Sri K.M. Koshy and Sri K.C. Sharma typed and retyped the text indefatigably. Shri K.C. Shah painstakingly prepared the maps.

The book, I sincerely hope, leads to a better understanding of the problems of the deprived, exploited and alienated segments of society and also better appreciation of the circumstances under which these sections are at times forced to rebel against the establishment and, in sheer desperation, even take up arms to uphold what they consider to be their minimum legitimate rights. I would consider my labours rewarded if this modest objective is achieved.

New Delhi
19.12.94

Prakash Singh

1

THE SPARK

STIRRINGS IN NAXALBARI

We can't forget them.
In their blood was the deluge of the tameless river
In their hands was the dream-
Higher than the skies.

—Avik Gangopadhyay

Naxalbari
March 3, 1967.

Three share-croppers, Lapa Kishan, Sangu Kishan and Ratia Kishan, supported by 150 CPI (M) followers, armed with lathis, bows and arrows and carrying party flags, lifted the entire stock of 300 mds. of paddy from the *jotedar's* granary without giving him any share.

A small incident in a small village. And yet it marked a turning point in the history of the Communist movement in India. What followed in the Naxalbari area comprising the three rural police stations of Naxalbari, Kharibari and Phansidewa was, according to Kanu Sanyal, "an armed struggle—not for land, but for state power"[1]. Soon Naxalbari became a national event. With Peking hailing this as "the front paw of the revolutionary armed struggle launched by the Indian people under the guidance of Mao Tse-tung" and boldly prognosticating that the spark "will start a prairie fire and will certainly set the vast expanses of India ablaze", Naxalbari assumed international significance. A new political philosophy based on Mao Tse-tung Thought was being applied to the Indian conditions. A new word was added to the political lexicon.

Naxalbari is strategically situated at the tri-junction of Nepal, Bangladesh (then East Pakistan) and India. The selection of the area indeed showed careful planning. China is not far off and thus there was a reliable hinterland. Nepal and the then East Pakistan could be used as sanctuaries to elude the police dragnet. Besides, the area, steeped as it was in the tradition of an aggressive peasant movement,

3

was ideal for building up an agrarian movement with political over-tones.

Naxalbari was, however, not the first peasant uprising to have taken place in India in recent times. In 1946, there was the Tebhaga (three parts) movement in undivided Bengal, which demanded reduction in the share of landlords from one-half of the crops to one-third. It spread from Dinajpur and Rangpur in the north to 24 Parganas in the south. The Kisan Sabhas, which were dominated by the Communist Party, encouraged the peasants to forcibly take away two-third of the harvested crops to their granaries. As a result, there were bloody clashes between the landlords and the peasants. The movement was essentially on economic demands, though in certain areas it led to the landlords fleeing away and the Kisan Sabhas establishing their sway over the villages. The movement petered out when the landlords, with the help of local administration, let loose a wave of repression. The Telengana insurrection (1946-1951) was much more broad-based and "has no parallel in Indian history since the 1857 war of independence"[2]. The peasants launched their struggle on economic issues against forced labour, illegal exactions and unauthorised evictions but it soon developed into an uprising against the feudal rule of the Nizam. The movement was directed by Communists from the very beginning and they mobilised large segments of people. It is said that the peasants were able to establish their control over about 3,000 villages and their influence extended over several others. Armed struggle continued even after the Indian troops had liberated Hyderabad, though the guerillas retreated to the forest areas to avoid any confrontation with the Army. A total of about 4,000 lives were lost in the prolonged struggle until it was formally withdrawn by the Communist Party. It was an important landmark in the history of peasant struggles in the subcontinent.

The Naxalbari uprising was a much smaller affair in comparison. Here the revolt lasted just 52 days—and that also because the state government prevaricated in the initial stages, and not more than a score of people were killed. But then Naxalbari "left a far-reaching impact on the entire agrarian scene throughout India. It was like the premeditated throw of a pebble bringing forth a series of ripples in the water".[3]

The total population of Naxalbari area then was 1,26,719, the tribals

4

constituting the most important segment. They included Santhals, Madesias, Oraons, Mundas, Rajbansis, etc. A large number of them had originally migrated from the Santhal Parganas of Bihar.

It is necessary to have a clear picture of the socio-economic conditions in the Naxalbari area for a proper understanding of the unrest and turmoil which followed. As per the Census Report of 1961, 57.7%, 72.2% and 64.5% of the total population of Naxalbari, Kharibari and Phansidewa respectively comprised Scheduled Castes and Tribes. They were engaged as cultivators, agricultural labour or employed in the tea gardens, forests and mines. The following figures illustrate the occupational pattern in the different police circles of the area.[4]

	Cultivators	Agricultural labour	Engaged in mining, forestry, plantation
	(%)	(%)	(%)
Naxalbari	37.5	4.6	40.0
Phansidewa	54.4	6.1	30.8
Kharibari	67.7	5.4	15.2

Lest an impression is created that agricultural labour formed a very small percentage, it must be clarified that the census data showed a peculiar inter-mingling of roles—a relatively high proportion of cultivators doubling up as agricultural labour and a good proportion of agricultural labour declaring 'cultivation' as their major secondary occupation.

	Proportion of cultivators with agricultural labour as secondary occupation	Proportion of agricultural labour with cultivation as secondary occupation
	(%)	(%)
Naxalbari	94.4	96.6
Phansidewa	76.5	96.2
Kharibari	92.6	58.8

The rural scene has to be viewed from another angle also. Not all the cultivators owned the holdings they ploughed; a significant proportion cultivated on agency basis (*bhagchash*). The following table lays bare the crux of the problem in the area—the extraordinary high percentage of *bhagchash* arrangement.

	Directly held	Held through agencies	Combinations
Naxalbari	37.1%	49.7%	13.2%
Phansidewa	39.4%	49.1%	11.5%
Kharibari	45.9%	33.9%	20.2%

Needless to say, the *bhagchasis* were exploited by the *jotedars*, and the threat of eviction always hung like the Damocles' sword over their heads. There were age-old agrarian disputes in the area in which the forces of *jotedars* were pitted against those of the land-hungry *kisans* and share-croppers. In 1953, the Government passed the Estates Acquisition Act, fixing the land ceiling at 25 acres of agricultural land, 15 acres of non-agricultural land and 5 acres of homestead land, making a total of 45 acres in all per head. This was followed, in 1955, by the Land Reforms Act. The *jotedars* thereafter started mala fide transfers of land. They sold land which actually vested in the Government; there were quite a few evictions also.

It was against this background that a peasant movement, spearheaded by the Kisan Sabha of the Communist Party of India, started in 1959 in the Naxalbari area where, in Gunnar Myrdal's words, "extreme tensions" had been built up. The movement did produce some results. Here and there lands were recovered and evictions registered a fall. The influence of the Kisan Sabha was, however, limited to parts of Naxalbari and Kharibari police stations. Besides, the movement suffered a setback in 1962 when, following the Chinese aggression, a number of leaders of the Kisan Sabha were arrested. It may be mentioned here that after the split in the Communist Party, the party cells in North Bengal were mostly captured by the CPI (Marxist). In the 1967 election, Jangal Santhal, President of the Siliguri sub-division Kisan Sabha, contested on a CPI(M) ticket and polled 10,484 votes (26%), second only to that of T. Wangdi of Congress, who was returned with 16,227 votes (41%).

The West Bengal State Kisan Conference held in October 1966 at Satgachia in Burdwan district was attended by eight delegates of the

Siliguri sub-division also, but they did not put forward any different opinions or oppose the official resolutions.[5] It was however obvious that the Siliguri militants, guided by Charu Mazumdar, had started veering on a different course. The propaganda leaflets brought out by them bore this out. One such leaflet of April 9, 1965 stated: "It is necessary now to come forward powerfully and tell the people forcefully that capturing of power area-wise is our way." It further gave a call for laying "the foundation of a new people's democratic India by building liberated *kisan* areas through *kisan* revolution." Another leaflet of August 30, 1966 bearing the caption 'Main task at present is to build real revolutionary party through uncompromising struggle against Revisionism' contained an exhortation to "organise partisan struggles" within six months. The Siliguri group, on return from Burdwan, organised a separate Kisan Convention. They gave a call to

i) Establish the authority of the peasant committees in all matters of the village,
ii) Get organised and be armed in order to crush the resistance of *jotedars* and rural reactionaries, and
iii) Smash the *jotedars'* monopoly of ownership of the land and redistribute the land anew through the peasant committees.[6]

It was like raising the battle-cry. The pattern of events which followed were mainly shaped by Charu Mazumdar, Kanu Sanyal and Jangal Santhal. Charu's was the brain, Kanu spread the organisational network, while Jangal mobilised the Santhals. They propagated that all the lands belonging to the *kulaks* would be taken away by the Government and would be available to the *kisans* if they became members of the Kisan Sabha. A nominal subscription of 20 paise for membership was fixed and the hard core started intimidating and even coercing the unwilling *kisans* to become members of the Sabha, the carrot held out being land for cultivation. In this way, a large number of Adivasis and Rajbansis were enlisted. Kanu Sanyal claimed that the membership of the Kisan Sabha jumped to nearly 40 thousand. The figure appears very much on the higher side, though the fact of increase in membership is undoubted. Sanyal also convinced the *kisans* that the United Front

Government of West Bengal would take no action against them in their struggle against the *kulaks*.

And so, what Peking called "a peal of spring thunder," crashed over North Bengal. The *People's Daily*, in its editorial of July 5, 1967 wrote:

> "Revolutionary peasants in the Darjeeling area have risen in rebellion. Under the leadership of a revolutionary group of the Indian Communist Party, a red area of rural revolutionary armed struggle has been established in India. This is a development of tremendous significance for the Indian people's revolutionary struggle.
>
> In the past few months, the peasant masses in the Darjeeling area led by the revolutionary group of the Indian Communist Party have thrown off the shackles of modern revisionism and smashed the trammels that bound them. They have seized grain, land and weapons from the landlords and plantation owners, punished the local tyrants and wicked gentry, and ambushed the reactionary troops and police that went to suppress them, thus demonstrating the powerful might of the peasants' revolutionary armed struggle. All imperialists, revisionists, corrupt officials, local tyrants and wicked gentry, and reactionary army and police are nothing in the eyes of the revolutionary peasants who are determined to strike them down to the dust. The revolutionary group of the Indian Communist Party have done the absolutely correct thing and they have done it well. The Chinese people joyfully applaud this revolutionary storm of the Indian peasants in the Darjeeling area as do all Marxist-Leninists and revolutionary people of the whole world".

The Santhals, armed with bows and arrows, forcibly occupied the lands of the *kulaks* and ploughed them to establish their ownership. Demonstrations were organised against persons holding paddy. In many cases, the entire stocks were lifted and distributed either amongst themselves or sold locally at cheaper rates. There were violent clashes. Between March and May 1967, nearly a hundred incidents were reported to the police; many more were not reported for fear of retaliatory action. The district authorities initially showed reluctance to grasp the nettle. They sought instructions from Calcutta on the plea that the tribals were armed and any stringent action by way

8

of raiding their hide-outs and arresting the wanted persons would lead to large scale violence. Hare Krishna Konar, Land Revenue Minister, flew to Siliguri on May 17 and succeeded in bringing Kanu Sanyal to the conference table at Sukhna forest bungalow in the foothills. Sanyal came on the specific assurance that he would not be arrested. It was agreed that lawless activities would be suspended, land distributed in consultation with the local agencies, stocks de-hoarded on the basis of information supplied by the people's committees and that all the wanted persons including Kanu Sanyal and Jangal Santhal would surrender to the police by a specified date. The Superintendent of Police was asked to submit a list of wanted persons to Sanyal at Hatigisha, a stronghold of the CPI (M), within two days. Kanu Sanyal did not turn up. The extremists backed out from the commitment and decided to continue their movement. The police meanwhile got instructions to arrest the persons wanted in connection with specific cases. On May 23, an armed police party led by Inspector Sonam Wangdi went to a village near Naxalbari police station to arrest some wanted persons. On his approach, the menfolk went into hiding, some of them taking positions with their bows and arrows behind the bushes. Wangdi left the armed squad at some distance and, accompanied by three others, went to persuade the womenfolk to surrender the wanted men without any trouble. While the dialogue was still going on, his body was riddled with three arrows. Wangdi died on the spot. The events of the following day further widened the hiatus between the authorities and the extremists. On May 24, two police parties, one led by the Superintendent of Police and the other by the Sub-Divisional Officer proceeded towards the village from different directions. Near Prasadjote, the SDO's party confronted a riotous mob which included women and children. The SDO thought he was being encircled and, in sheer panic, ordered the police to open fire. Ten persons were killed, six of them being women.

The situation thereafter progressively deteriorated. There were cases of murder, dacoity, looting of property and theft of arms and ammunition. The extremists moved about freely at the head of Santhal groups, armed with bows and arrows. On June 10, a mob of about 150 men carrying CPI (M) flags raided the house of *jotedar* Nagen Roy Choudhary in PS Kharibari and looted paddy, ornaments and

9

a double barrel gun. They also abducted Nagen Roy Choudhary and subsequently murdered him. It is said that a *panchayat* presided over by Kanu Sanyal had earlier passed death sentence on him as the *jotedar* had dared to organise a resistance group. The same day, another gang raided the house of Jainandan Singh in village Baramanijote, Police Station Naxalbari and decamped with his double barrel gun, 25 cartridges and some valuables.

It was obvious that firm action was called for to tackle the situation. On July 5, after a good deal of dithering, the West Bengal Cabinet decided in favour of police action. However, it was only on July 12 that the police operations commenced. There was no resistance worth the name and the movement was squashed with unexpected case. About 700 persons were arrested[7]. The police success was due partly to the massive show of strength—nearly 1500 policemen were deployed—and partly to the harrying tactics of constant raids which kept the extremists running from pillar to post. Jangal Santhal was utterly famished and in low spirits when arrested on August 10; he had not had any meal for the last two days.

What did Naxalbari achieve? Kanu Sanyal's report on the 'Peasant Movement in the Terai Region' makes a rather tall claim. It says that the peasants were able to accomplish "ten great tasks": (1) the old feudal structure which had existed for centuries was smashed; (2) fraudulent deeds and documents were burnt; (3) unequal agreements between the peasants and the *jotedars* were all declared null and void; (4) hoarded rice was confiscated; (5) open trials of tyrannical *jotedars* were held; (6) goonda elements attached to the *jotedars* were suitably dealt with; (7) armed groups of peasants were organised with traditional weapons and guns snatched from the *jotedars*; (8) night watch was arranged to maintain law and order; (9) revolutionary committees were set up to establish peasants' political power; and (10) the existing bourgeois laws and courts were declared inoperative.[8]

Samar Sen assessed the Naxalbari uprising in the following words:

"Naxalbari exploded many a myth and restored faith in the courage and character of the revolutionary Left in India. It seemed that the ever-yawning gap between precept and practice since Telengana would be bridged. Indeed, the upheaval was such that nothing remained the same after Naxalbari. People had to readjust their position vis-a-vis every aspect of the system: political, administrative, military, cultural."[9]

According to another critic, "Naxalbari marked an advance for the people of India as the Paris Commune had marked an advance for the world proletariat."[10] At the other extreme is the rather harsh verdict of Pannalal Das Gupta: "The Naxalbari 'revolution' is at best a caricature of what Mao Tse-tung did and taught for twenty years of protracted revolution in China. Even compared to what the Santhals did in their Santhal revolt in the middle of the nineteenth century or what the indigo-peasants did against the planters, the performances of the Naxalbari revolutionaries was a hollow imitation."

The failure of the movement in Naxalbari was attributed by its leaders to (1) lack of a strong party organisation, (2) failure to build a powerful mass base, (3) ignorance of military affairs, and (4) a formal attitude towards land reforms.[11] Kanu Sanyal deplored the absence of a party armed with the theory of Marxism-Leninism and "its highest development in the present era—Mao Tse-tung's Thought". The failure to rely on the people and build a powerful mass base also prevented the struggle from rising to a higher stage. In a self-critical vein, Kanu Sanyal observed: "We did not realise that it is the people who make history, that they are the real heroes". The petty bourgeois leadership imposed itself upon the people and set limits on how far the peasant masses could go. "This resulted in thwarting the initiative of the masses". The ignorance of military affairs was another contributory factor. It was felt that they had, in the first stage of the struggle, under-estimated the enemy's strength and indulged in idle day-dreaming. The result was that when police action commenced, the Naxalites found themselves in disarray and the movement started petering out. The failure to establish revolutionary political power and carry out land reforms further blunted the edge of class struggle. The peasants had formed central and zonal revolutionary committees and seized land from the *jotedars*, but they turned these two achievements into a most formal affair. The party did not carry out the task of political education among the masses and paid inadequate attention to the question of re-distribution of land.

11

In April 1973, nearly six years after the Naxalbari uprising, Kanu Sanyal came out with a more objective assessment and attributed the failure to ignoring the socio-political conditions of the Indian people. In an article entitled *More About Naxalbari*, he wrote:

"The immaturity of grasping Marxism-Leninism and Mao Tse-tung Thought in the concrete condition of India is the sole reason as to why such a long time was required to understand the importance of the Naxalbari peasant uprising. So, extreme price had to be paid through heavy losses.

India is a vast and ancient land of many nations. Failure to keep in view the specific features of Indian society and inability to solve the problems of Indian revolution from the traditions of struggles of the Indian people led to subjective super-imposing of the experiences of other countries mechanically; it brought about right and left deviation in the Indian Communist movement. Expressed in the language of Mao Tse-tung, it is 'cutting the feet to fit the shoes'. Denying the materialist truth that it is the Indian people who are the real creators of Indian history since time immemorial, the communist leadership painted some persons of the ruling classes of different era as creators of history and father of the nation."[12]

The Naxalbari uprising did not achieve much by itself but is nevertheless a watershed in the history of the Indian Communist movement. Its importance is symbolic. Here was an insurrection which challenged head-on the existing order. Here was a movement aimed at transforming the society. Here was an uprising blessed by Peking. From Naxalbari the sparks flew all over the country, and there was political upheaval.

2

THE FLAME

2.1 A NEW PARTY IS BORN

If there is to be revolution, there must be
a revolutionary party.

-Mao

The Naxalbari uprising placed the CPI(M) leadership in West Bengal on the horns of a dilemma. It was torn between its consideration for the party workers pursuing a militant line in Darjeeling district and its responsibility for maintaining law and order in the State. Ultimately, the mounting pressure from the coalition partners and the hue and cry in the public forced CPI(M)'s hands and it ordered police action against the Naxalbari revolutionaries. This action, however, caused consternation among the party rank and file. The dissidents alleged that Naxalbari had "stripped naked" the leadership of the CPI(M) mouthing revolutionary slogans and laid bare before the people "the utter hollowness of their revolutionism". The Politburo of the CPI(M) took cognizance of the discordant notes and decided to enforce discipline. It announced that those deviating from the party line would be expelled, and the state committees were instructed to take action against the extremist elements accordingly. The organisational measures were reinforced by an ideological offensive against the extremists. The Central Committee of the party, which met at Madurai from August 18 to 27, 1967, accused the extremists of "neglecting all the immediate tasks of mobilising the class and relying on spontaneity."[1] It denounced the left deviation as an "ideological disease of frustrated individuals"[2] and condemned the Naxalbari line as "wrong, disruptive and anti-Marxist-Leninist."[3]

The Central Committee also adopted a resolution on 'Divergent views between our Party and the CPC' in view of the fact that extremist elements were getting inspiration and encouragement from Peking. In it the CPI(M) expressed differences with the Communist Party of

China on the following vital issues connected with the Communist movement in the world in general and in India in particular:

a) The CPC's outright rejection of the principle of unity in action among different socialist states and the world communist parties against imperialism on the ground that some of these socialist states and communist parties were under the leadership of revisionists was considered wrong in principle and harmful in practice.

b) The CPI(M) did not subscribe to the "erroneous theory" of US-Soviet collaboration for the sharing of world hegemony and perpetuation of world domination even though it believed in exposing the class collaborationist and revisionist policies of the leaders of Soviet Union.

c) The CPI(M) considered the CPC's reading of class relations in India and its assessment of the current situation and the tactical line worked out on that basis as completely incorrect and contrary to the realities.[4]

The CPI(M) felt that these mistakes assumed all the more grievous proportions in view of the CPC's interference in the internal affairs of the party with a view to imposing its own political line on the latter. The Central Committee quoted from the Chinese Communist Party's letter of June 14, 1963 to the Communist Party of Soviet Union, saying that it was "impermissible for any party to place itself above others to interfere in their internal affairs and to adopt patriarchal ways in relation with them",[5] and deplored that the Chinese leaders did not deem it necessary to take up their differences with the CPI(M) on party-to-party level before applauding the extremists of Naxalbari as real revolutionaries. The debate within the CPI(M) was given the stamp of finality at Burdwan, where an All India Plenum was held in April 1968. The ideological document, as finally adopted, rejected the concept of peaceful co-existence, peaceful economic competition and peaceful transition as interpreted and practised by the CPSU on the ground that it amounted to class collaboration and conciliation on the global plane.[6] It interpreted the concept of peaceful co-existence as a concept of "respite" to be correctly utilised to consolidate the socialist state economically, politically and militarily so that imperialist aggression could be successfully met and the imperialists vanquished.

It rejected, however, the Chinese formulation that the USSR had become an ally of imperialism and was working for sharing world's hegemony with American imperialism and for the division of spheres of influence in the world.

The extremsits retorted with no less vehemence. Charu Mazumdar alleged that the party's Central Committee meeting had "dragged down the party to the level of a revisionist bourgeois party," and declared that under the circumstances Marxist-Leninists were left with no alternative but "to declare war"[7] against those policies. He insinuated that the Central Committee had become an ally and friend of American imperialism, Soviet revisionism and the Indian reactionary government. The *Liberation* of May 1968 aptly summed up the extremists' bitterness.

> "The Naxalbari peasant revolt exposed the counter revolutionary character of this neo-revisionist clique....Burdwan has completed the unmasking of these agents of reaction who masquerade as Marxists."

Charu Mazumdar took the stand that Mao Tse-tung Thought is the "highest form of Marxism-Leninism" and that agrarian revolution is the only path for the liberation of the country. Such a revolution could be brought about by building up revolutionary bases in the rural areas, encircling the urban centres by expanding these bases, and organising people's liberation forces from among the peasant guerilla formations.

The extremists were all the time conscious of the need to have a revolutionary party. The first step towards organisational consolidation of the extremists was taken in November 1967 with the formation of an All India Coordination Committee at a meeting held in Calcutta which was attended by extremists from different states. The extremist leaders were of the view that there was an excellent revolutionary situation in the country with all the classical symptoms as enunciated by Lenin. They criticised the CPI(M) for having betrayed the cause of Indian revolution and chosen the path of parliamentarism and class-collaboration. The Coordination Committee was entrusted with the following tasks:

a) To develop and coordinate militant and revolutionary struggles at

17

all levels, specially peasant struggles of the Naxalbari type under the leadership of the working class;

b) To develop militant, revolutionary struggles of the working class and other toiling people to combat economism and to orient these struggles towards agrarian revolution;

c) To wage an uncompromising ideological struggle against revisionism and neo-revisionism and to popularise Mao Tse-tung's Thought, which is Marxism-Leninism of the present era, and to unite on that basis all revolutionary elements within and outside the party; and

d) To undertake preparation of a revolutionary programme and tactical line based on concrete analysis of the Indian situation in the light of Mao Tse-tung's Thought.[8]

Six months later, in May 1968, the Coordination Committee met again. It decided to issue a new Declaration and change its name to All India Coordination Committee of Communist Revolutionaries (AICCCR). The Declaration underscored the semi-colonial and semi-feudal character of India and gave a call for People's Democratic Revolution. The revolution could be accomplished by (i) overthrowing the "four mountains" of U.S. imperialism, Soviet revisionism, big Indian landlords and comprador-bureaucrat bourgeoisie which were weighing heavily on the back of the toiling people; (ii) setting up revolutionary base areas in the countryside; (iii) establishing the leadership of the working class; and (iv) encircling the cities from the countryside with a view to capturing them. The Declaration reiterated the great importance which the extremists attached to Mao's Thought; they called it the "acme of Marxism-Leninism in our era". Charu Mazumdar emphatically declared that the People's Democratic Revolution in India could be led to a victorious finale only on the basis of Mao's Thought. "The extent to which one assimilates and applies the Thought of the Chairman will determine whether one is a revolutionary or not"[9]. The AICCCR also adpted a resolution on the boycott of election which was denounced as a "sinister counter-revolutionary manoeuvre of the reactionary ruling classes and their lackeys."[10] It was said that the parliamentary path would blunt their revolutionary consciousness and disrupt the class struggle.

The third meeting of the Communist Revolutionaries held in October 1968 expressed the view that the Naxalbari peasant struggle had entered the second stage—the stage of guerilla war—and drew satisfaction from the fact that in several areas of UP, Bihar, Madhya Pradesh and Andhra Pradesh armed struggles had broken out under the inspiration of the Naxalbari movement. It gave a call for building up revolutionary bases in the countryside and emphasised that this should be their major task in the coming period. It also adopted resolutions hailing the people and the Communist Party of China for the success of the proletarian cultural revolution, expressing indignation at the, "dastardly act of imperialist invasion of Czechoslovakia by the Soviet revisionist renegade clique and greeting the people of Albania on their renouncing and withdrawing from the Warsaw Pact."[11]

In November 1968, there were incidents of attacks on police stations in Kerala. These were to have a bearing on the unity of the extremist movement. It so happened that the ultras of Kunnikal Narayanan group attacked two police stations at Tellicherry and Calicut and a wireless station at Pulpally. A sub-inspector was wounded and a wireless operator was speared to death. Later on, it transpired that the extremists had organised a training camp in an adjoining area where plans of attacks on the police stations were drawn up. These attacks were to be followed by similar attacks on big landlords and attempts at securing firearms. The interpretations given to the incident by the AICCCR and its Andhra unit headed by Nagi Reddy exacerbated their differences and eventually led to their parting of the ways. The differences were indeed on basic issues. The first and foremost was the question of loyalty to the Communist Party of China. The AICCCR considered Nagi Reddy's press statement criticising Kerala extremists' attack on the police stations even after the Chinese Communist Party had endorsed them as clear proof that Nagi Reddy and the Andhra Committee were not loyal to the CPC. Secondly, there was the question of attitude to the Srikakulam struggle. The AICCCR felt that the Andhra Committee, instead of owning and clarifying the movement, merely accorded it lukewarm support. And thirdly, they disagreed on the issue of boycott of elections. Nagi Reddy did not comply with the AICCCR's direction to resign from the Andhra State Assembly within a specified period. The AICCCR therefore disaffiliated the Andhra Coordination

Committee, though it agreed to treat the latter as "friends and comrades outside the Coordination"[12] and decided to maintain non-antagonistic relations with them.

The AICCR leaders, at their next meeting held on February 8, 1969, expressed impatience over the delay in the formation of a revolutionary party. They felt that the Coordination Committee had served a useful purpose but it could not fulfil "the complex political and organisational tasks arising out of the present stage of revolutionary struggles." It was, therefore, essential to form an all India party of all the revolutionaries. "Without a revolutionary party, there can be no revolutionary discipline and without revolutionary discipline the struggles cannot be raised to a higher level."[13] Some extremist leaders were however of the opionion that it would be proper to form a party only after the opportunist tendencies and trends were purged through class struggles. This was dubbed as an idealist deviation and it was said that "to conceive of a party without contradictions, without the struggle between the opposites, i.e. to think of a pure and faultless party is indulging in mere idealist fantasy."[14] Mao's statement that "if there were no contradictions in the party and no ideological struggles to resolve them, the party's life would come to an end," was also quoted to buttress the argument in favour of early formation of a Marxist-Leninist party.

There are strong reasons to believe that the Communist Party of China also, around this time, conveyed instructions for the formation of a third Communist Party in the country. Charu Mazumdar in an article *Why Must We Form the Party Now?* clearly mentioned that "the international leadership has been reminding us time and again of the importance of building up a party". Earlier, Sanmugathasan, Politburo Member of the Communist Part of Ceylon, on return from China, where he had an interview with Mao Tse-tung, expressed the view that the political and economic situation prevailing in India was almost tailor-made for revolution and the only thing lacking was a genuine revolutionary leadership based on Marxism-Leninism and the Thought of Mao Tse-tung.[15]

On April 22,1969, the one hundredth birth anniversary of Lenin, the All India Coordination Committee of Communist Revolutionaries declared its own liquidation and the formation of the Communist Party of India (Marxist-Leninist) based on the Thoughts of Mao Tse-tung. A Central Organising Committee of the party was constituted. The extremist movement thus acquired an organisational and ideological base after groping for nearly two years. A number of splinter extremist groups continued to exist, but the CPI(ML) gradually emerged as the most important component of the extremist movement in the country.

The formation of the CPI(ML), it has been said, was a historical necessity because the CPI and the CPI(M) had degenerated into "social-chauvinist bourgeois parties, anxious to defend the present system and to serve the ruling classes faithfully."[16] Besides, as Mao had said, "if there is to be revolution, there must be a revolutionary party."

The political resolution of the CPI(ML)[17] indicated the party's assessment of the prevailing conditions in India and its attitude to the various problems. These were briefly as follows:

i) India is a semi-colonial and semi-feudal country, the Indian state is a state of the big landlords and comprador-bureaucrat capitalists and its government is a lackey of US imperialism and Soviet social-imperalism.

ii) The principal contradiction in the country is between feudalism and the peasant masses.

iii) The Indian revolution is at the stage of People's Democratic Revolution, the main content of which is agrarian revolution.

iv) The revolutionary situation in India is excellent with the ruling classes enmeshed in economic and political crisis. The contradictions between imperialism and the people, between feudalism and peasants, between capital and labour and between different sections of the ruling classes are growing sharper everyday.

v) The party would strive to build a united front of all revolutionary classes on the basis of alliance between workers and peasants.

vi) Guerilla warfare would be the basic tactic of struggle.

The resolution on party organisation[18] stated in unambiguous terms that the CPI(ML) would be a party of armed revolution. "No other path exists before the Indian people but the path of armed revolution". It would also be a rural-based party:

"...the first and foremost task of our Party is to rouse the peasant

21

masses in the countryside to wage guerilla war, unfold agrarian revolution, build rural base, use the countryside to encircle the cities and finally to capture the cities and to liberate the whole country. Thus, in the present day phase of Indian Revolution, the centre of gravity of our work has to be in the villages."

The party, it was clarified, would function with utmost secrecy and keep its main cadres underground. Quoting Lin Biao, it was said that "guerilla warfare is the only way to mobilise and apply the whole strength of the people against the enemy." This formulation, as we shall see later, was to land the party in a quandry when Lin Biao was disgraced in China. For the present, however, the party workers were directed to concentrate on "developing guerilla forms of armed struggle and not waste time and its energies in holding open mass meetings and forming *kisan sabhas* in the old style." The Marxist-Leninist Party, it was also said, would be the party of new style in the sense that it would integrate theory with practice and criticism with self-criticism.

Kanu Sanyal, the fire-brand Naxalite leader, announced the formation of the CPI(ML) at a rally held in Calcutta on May 1, 1969. He claimed that the revolutionary situation was ripe both at home and abroad with Mao Tse-tung at the helm of the world revolution being led by the Communist Party of China. The new party, he asserted, will be able to make "a new sun and a new moon shine in the sky of our great motherland."[19]

Significantly, the rally was preceded by violent clashes between Naxalites and supporters of the United Front. Bombs, crackers, pipe-guns and brickbats were freely used in the clashes. About 200 persons were injured, 50 of them seriously. It was a precursor of the shape of things to come.

The CPI(ML) was ironically beset with internal rifts from the very beginning. Some members of the AICCCR felt that the decision to form a party had been taken in great haste and in an undemocratic manner without eliciting the views of all the units of the Committee. Parimal Das Gupta, General Secretary of the State Electricity Board Employees Union, defected and formed a rival Coordination Committee at the state-level. He criticised CPI(ML)'s method of guerilla warfare as 'Che Guevarism' and faulted it for ignoring the task of building mass organisations and not participating in trade unions. Another important leader, Asit Sen, who actually presided over the rally where the formation of the CPI(ML) was announced but was unaware of the decision till the last moment, also parted company with the CPI(ML).

At the international level, the formation of the CPI(ML) was welcomed by the Chinese Communist Party, which published the party's political resolution in *People's Daily*. Peking Radio welcomed the event. Recognition also came from the Marxist-Leninist groups of other countries like U.K., Albania and Sri Lanka. The CPI(ML) acknowledged its gratitude to these fraternal parties:

> "We Marxist-Leninists in India owe a deep debt of gratitude to Marxist-Leninists in other countries, especially to the great Communist Party of China, the leader of the international communist movement, for their warm fraternal support and correct guidance at every crisis in our party history. We remember how the heroic struggle of the Naxalbari peasantry, the first single spark of the Indian revolution, was applauded by the great party led by Chairman Mao. Now, too, the great CPC has come forward to extend its unmistakable and inspiring support to our new-born party, the party of armed struggle based on Marxism-Leninism-Mao Tsetung Thought."[20]

In due course, the CPI(ML) developed a close nexus with the Marxist-Leninist parties of these countries and also with others like Australia, USA, Canada, Cuba, Indonesia, Italy, Nepal and East Pakistan. The Chinese continued to extend ideological guidance and material assistance to the CPI(ML) until they got disenchanted with Charu Mazumdar's tactical aberrations. Financial help and propaganda literature were liberally provided. The Chinese also directed the underground 'Naga Federal Government', which was getting substantial weaponry from China during this period, to coordinate their insurgency with that of the Naxalites and, with this end in view, give them arms and ammunition. The Naga rebels accordingly gave one LMG and ten rifles to the Naxalites in Assam. The Communist Party of Great Britain(ML) remitted £1000 to Suniti Kumar Ghosh, Central Committee member, soon after the party was formed. A party delegation visited Albania in October 1969 and held discussions with Enver Hoxha, Secretary-General of the Albanian Party of Labour. Sanmugathasan, Secretary of the Ceylonese Communist Party, was used by Peking to convey its views on policy matters to the CPI(ML). Eastern Nepal was used by the Naxalites as a sanctuary. From East Pakistan, the EPCP(ML) sent a message of greetings to the CPI(ML) Party Congress and acknowledged that the guerilla warfare being waged in India had provided inspiration and taught many lessons to the cadres in East Pakistan.

The CPI(ML) indeed functioned as a contingent of the international Communist movement.

2.2   IDEAS THAT IGNITED

The important thing is the revolution, the
revolutionary cause, revolutionary ideas,
revolutionary objectives, revolutionary sentiments,
revolutionary virtues.

—Fidel Castro

The Naxalite movement had a meteoric phase for about two years from the formation of the party in May 1969 till the end of June 1971. The ripples starting from Naxalbari spread in ever-widening circles to practically all parts of the country. The only areas which remained untouched were the North-Eastern states and the Union Territories of Goa, Pondicherry and Andaman & Nicobar Islands. The dominant strand of the movement was the annihilation of class enemies. It was Charu Mazumdar's distinctive contribution to the movement. It was his triumph as well as his tragedy—triumph because it achieved a considerable measure of success in the initial stages when several *jotedars* fled from the countryside and there were tremors among all shades of oppressors, and tragedy because the killings, not always discriminate, alienated the general mass of people and, further, there were serious ideological differences within the party which weakened and fragmented the movement.

The annihilation of class enemies was directed at not merely the physical liquidation of a few hated landlords and usurers but at the "overthrow of the feudal class in an area economically, politically and militarily."[1] It was explained that after the class enemies were annihilated, others of his ilk would also flee in utter panic and the area would be freed of the class enemies and their agents. This would raise the armed struggle to a higher plane. Annihilation of class enemies was thus a "higher form of class struggle and the beginning of guerilla war." The annihilation campaign had other advantages also. It raised—

25

at least that was the claim—the political consciousness of the people and created conditions for the emergence of a new type of man who feared neither hardship nor death. "The battle of annihilation liberates the people not only from the oppression of the landlord class and the state but also liberates them from the shackles of backward ideas and removes from the minds of the people poisonous weeds of self-interest, clan interest, localism, casteism, religious superstition, etc."[2]

The class enemies included landlords and their agents, rich peasants, money-lenders and police informers. The poor and landless peasants were relied upon to carry on this campaign. Squads of poor and landless peasants, imbued with the politics of seizure of political power by armed force and burning with class hatred, annihilated the feudal oppressors.

What weapons were to be used for annihilations? Here, as on several other points, the Naxalites took the cue from Mao. "Weapons are an important factor in war, but not the decisive factor; it is people, not things that are decisive." The party workers were therefore advised to rely on conventional weapons like choppers, spears, javelines and sickles. The tendency to acquire guns and other firearms was discouraged on the ground that even if they managed to get hold of a few guns, they would not be able to retain them and those would inevitably fall into the hands of the police. The party's thinking in the matter was expressed by the Debra Organising Committee of the CPI(ML) in the following words:

> "The guerillas are used to bows and arrows and not guns, and so, their initiative and inventiveness develop in using the former. Our tactic, plan and choice of weapons should be such as can unleash the initiative of the masses. As they realize the limitations of their primitive weapons, in course of struggle, they themselves will take initiative to procure modern weapons, which will then not be a hindrance to releasing the initiative of the masses but will, on the contrary, become its complement."[3]

The act of annihilation of class enemies was considered by the Naxalites to be the "primary stage of the guerilla struggle." It is therefore necessary to understand the CPI(ML)'s concept of guerilla struggle.

26

It was explained by Charu Mazumdar that "guerilla warfare is and will remain the basic form of struggle for the entire period of the democratic revolution."[4] He was at pains to distinguish the CPI(ML)'s concept of guerilla war from that advocated by Che Guevara in which guerilla war was waged by the petty bourgeois intelligentsia without the support of the peasant masses. He underscored that the guerilla war, as understood by the Naxalites in India, was initiated by the class conscious elements of the poor and landless peasants and that it could be led and carried on only with their active cooperation. Another point of difference from Guevara type of guerilla warfare was that there was no reliance on firearms and the peasant masses depended exclusively on primitive weapons conveniently available to them. The guerilla war, according to Charu Mazumdar, could be started wherever there were peasants. It was a mistaken understanding that such warfare could be started only in mountainous area or in jungles. Another point—and this led to divergence of opinion in the party circles—stressed by Mazumdar was that mass movements and mass organisations were not necessary pre-conditions for waging guerilla warfare. On the contrary, these mass movements and mass organisations exposed the revolutionary workers before the enemy and were therefore obstacles in the way of development and expansion of guerilla warfare. What was indispensable was the spreading and propagation of revolutionary politics or the Thought of Mao Tse-tung.

The *Liberation* of February 1970 gives an expose of Charu Mazumdar's views on guerilla actions. It was stressed that complete secrecy must be observed in forming a guerilla unit. "The method of forming a guerilla unit has to be wholly conspiratorial. No inkling of such a conspiracy should be given out even in the meetings of the political units of the party. This conspiracy should be between individuals and on a person to person basis. The petty bourgeois intellectual comrade must take the initiative in this respect as far as possible. He should approach the poor peasant who, in his opinion, has the most revolutionary potential and whisper in his ears. 'Don't you think it is a good thing to finish off such and such a *jotedar*?' This is how the guerillas had to be selected and recruited singly and in secret and organised into a unit."

The guerilla unit must be small, well-knit and mobile. It should

27

generally not have more than seven members and the unit should be led by a commander. Before undertaking any action, a thorough investigation of the target should be done by keeping watch over his movements so that the best possible time and place for attack is chosen. Shelters should be arranged with the utmost care and caution. These should be spread and located in different villages far from the place where the guerilla action is to take place. A detailed plan of operation should be worked out in consultation with the petty bourgeois intellectual comrade. At the time of attack, the guerillas should come from different directions, pretending to be innocent persons and gather at a previously appointed place where they should wait for the class enemy. After the annihilation is carried out, the guerillas should disperse to their respective shelters. This should be followed by propaganda activity. The political cadres, pretending to be neutral, would start a whisper campaign like this: "So, that devil of a man has got killed after all, good riddance, eh! Can't find enough words to praise those who have done it. They have done a heroic thing, haven't they? Wish they would carry on with this business until the whole pack of those blood-suckers is finished off. Oh, how fine will be everything then; just think, when they are gone all this area will belong to us, all this land, all this crops, all the riches will be ours; because, once these scoundrels are gone how can the police know who is tilling whose land?"[5] After the masses begin to respond to such propaganda, the political cadre would gradually become bolder and hold group meetings. At this stage, the petty bourgeois intellectual would also come out of hiding and hold meetings to rouse the masses. The guerilla units thereafter find out new targets and work out new plans of action. The process thus goes on until Red Terror is firmly established.

While expounding the above principles of guerilla action, however, Charu Mazumdar's enthusiasm overran his discretion and he made the fantastic statement that "he who has not dipped his hand in the blood of class enemies can hardly be called a Communist." The statement caused a furore among the party leaders and was subsequently disapproved even by the Chinese leadership.

The guerilla warfare was, in turn, to lead to the establishment of base areas. A base area was one where the feudal regime of the landlord

28

had been destroyed and the revolutionary authority of the peasants established.

These ideas fired the imagination of party workers and sympathisers—and the Naxalite movement surged stridently. The ideological formulations, however, had inherent flaws which, in due course, led not only to the movement losing its momentum but the party also getting splintered. The annihilation campaign, it has been rightly said, had four basic objectives:[6]

i)   smash the feudal authority in the villages and replace it by the authority of the peasants;
ii) establish 'red terror' as opposed to the 'white terror' of feudal elements;
iii) arouse the poor sections of the rural masses to take over the leadership of the movement; and
iv) encourage the common people to shake off their fear and inertia to join the Naxalites.

Not that these objectives were not achieved to a certain extent, but Mazumdar failed to visualise the devastating implications of his flawed approach for the very cause he was trying to champion. Mass movements were neglected, economic struggles did not get due attention and 'white terror' was provoked to launch fierce counter-attacks which nearly decimated the Naxalites. The movement did not have the vital ingredients to sustain itself. No wonder, after attaining a certain trajectory, it showed a sharp downward trend.

At the end of 1969, Charu Mazumdar summed up the lessons of the year in the following words:

> "Rely on the poor and landless peasants; educate them in Mao Tse-tung Thought; adhere firmly to the path of armed struggle; build guerilla force and march forward along the path of liquidating the class enemies; only thus can the high tide of struggle advance irresistibly."[7]

He also expressed his optimism that the year 1970 held the promise of still bigger victories. A month later, Charu Mazumdar gave the call for making the 1970s 'the decade of liberation' and exhorted the party workers to "spread the sparks of this revolutionary armed struggle throughout India, here and now."

The holding of the first Party Congress by the CPI(ML) in the middle of May 1970 was an important landmark in the evolution of Naxalite movement in the country. The Party Congress was held in underground conditions in Calcutta and was attended by delegates from the various states of India. It clearly acknowledged its links with the Chinese Communist Party in a resolution conveying "revolutionary greetings to Chairman Mao Tse-tung to whose all conquering Thought and to whom personally our Party owes its birth and phenomenal growth." The Congress did not mince its words in recording that "our Party and revolution have received and are receiving the personal care and guidance of Chairman Mao." Through another resolution, the Party gave a call to avenge the death of "great martyrs" by intensifying the armed class struggle and the war of annihilation of class enemies. The party workers were advised to turn their grief into burning class hatred.

The Congress adopted the Party Programme, the Political Organisational Report, the Party Constitution and elected the Central Committee. The salient features of the party programme were:[8]

1. India achieved a 'sham independence' in 1947, when Congress leadership representing the comprador-bourgeoisie and big landlords was installed to power;
2. the Indian people are now weighed down under "four huge mountains" namely US imperialism, Soviet social imperialism, feudalism and comprador-bureaucrat capital;
3. the contradiction between feudalism and the broad masses of the Indian people is the principal contradiction of the present phase;
4. the present Indian society is semi-feudal and semi-colonial in character;
5. the government has been suppressing the genuine rights of all the nationalities and national and religious minorities like Kashmiris, Nagas and Mizos who are being denied the right of self-determination;
6. the foreign policy of the country serves the interests of imperialism, social-imperialism and reaction;

7. the country is in the stage of democratic revolution, the essence of which is agrarian revolution;
8. the revolution will establish the dictatorship of the working class, the peasantry, the petty bourgeoisie and even a section of the small and middle bourgeoisie under the leadership of the working class which is the most organised, advanced detachment of the people;
9. a Democratic Front would be built up under the leadership of the working class and it would include the landless and poor peasants, the middle peasants and also a section of the rich peasants with the urban petty bourgeoisie and the revolutionary intellectuals as reliable allies; and
10. India's liberation would be achieved by people's war, which would involve creating small bases of armed struggle all over the country by waging guerilla warfare.

The party also outlined the major tasks which the People's Democratic State would carry out. These deserve to be quoted *in extenso*:[9]

a) Confiscation of all the banks and enterprises of foreign capital and liquidation of all imperialist debt.
b) Confiscation of all the enterprises of the comprador-bureaucrat capitalists.
c) Confiscation of all land belonging to the landlords and their re-distribution among the landless and poor peasants on the principle of land to the tillers; cancellation of all debts of the peasantry and other toiling people. All facilities necessary for development of agriculture to be guaranteed.
d) Enforce eight hours a day, increase wages, institute unemployment relief and social insurance, remove all inequalities on the basis of equal pay for equal work.
e) Improve the living conditions of soldiers and give land and job to the ex-servicemen.
f) Enforce better living conditions of the people and remove unemployment.
g) Develop new democratic culture in place of colonial and feudal culture.
h) Abolish the present educational system and educational institu-

tions and build up a new educational system and new educational institutions consistent with the needs of People's Democratic India.

i) Abolish the caste system, remove all social inequalities and discrimination on religious grounds and guarantee equality of status to women.

j) Unify India and recognise the right of self-determination.

k) Give equal status to all national languages.

l) Abolish all exorbitant taxes and miscellaneous assessments and adopt a consolidated progressive tax system.

m)People's political power to be exercised through Revolutionary People's Councils at all levels.

n) Alliance to be formed with the international proletariat and the oppressed nations of the world under the leadership of the CPC.

The political-organisational report[10] adopted at the Party Congress claimed that peasants' armed struggle under the leadership of the CPI(ML) had spread far and wide and engulfed twelve states of the country. It gave a call for strengthening the party, which was declared the "most important, most immediate and most sacred task of the revolutionary people of India." The Party expressed its resolve to continue the annihilation campaign in a more determined and concerted way and "develop the struggles in mighty waves."

Charu Mazumdar's speech on the political-organisational report[11] at the Party Congress for the first time indicated that differences were brewing inside the Party over the issues of (a) annihilation, (b) use of firearms and (c) dependence on the petty bourgeois intellectual. Charu Mazumdar made a virulent attack on the dissidents whom he dubbed as "centrists" and made a vigorous defence of the party line. He said that without class struggle—the battle of annihilation—the initiative of the poor peasant masses cannot be released, the political consciousness of the fighters cannot be raised, the new man cannot emerge and the people's army cannot be created. On the question of firearms, he argued that their use at this stage, instead of releasing the initiative of the peasant masses, would stifle it.

"If guerilla fighters start the battle of annihilation with their conventional weapons, the common landless and poor peasants would come forward with bare hands and join the battle of annihilation. A common landless peasant, ground down by age-old repression, will see the light and avenge himself on the class enemy. His initiative will be released. In this way, the peasant masses will join the guerilla fighters, their revolutionary enthusiasm will know no bounds and a mighty wave of people's upsurge will sweep the country. After the initiative of the peasant masses to annihilate the class enemy with bare hands or home-made weapons has been released and the peasants revolutionary power has been established, they should take up the guns and face the world."

Charu Mazumdar felt that "there is the possibility of a tremendous upsurge in India," and he therefore called upon the cadres to start as many points of armed struggle as possible instead of confining it. "Expand anywhere and everywhere" was his message. Such expansions were particularly noticeable in Srikakulam in Andhra Pradesh, Debra-Gopiballavpur in West Bengal, Mushahari in Bihar and Palia in Lakhimpur district of UP.

3

THE FIRE

3.1   ANDHRA PRADESH—SRIKAKULAM

Dignitaries fell,
wrapped in their togas
of worm-eaten mud,
nameless people shouldered spears,
tumbled the walls,
nailed the tyrant to his golden door .
                                        —Pablo Neruda

"Srikakulam is an immortal name, a great hope. Srikakulam is the future history of India. Srikakulam will be the bulwark of revolution." This is how Charu Mazumdar assessed the Girijan insurgency in Srikakulam. The movement in Srikakulam actually predates Naxalbari. It started as early as 1961. Besides, the Naxalites here achieved a considerable measure of success and were able to carve out a 'Red Area' where the writ of the government did not run, even if for a small period only. And yet, for inexplicable reasons, the movement in Srikakulam has not been given as much importance as the movement in West Bengal.

Srikakulam is in the north-eastern region of Andhra Pradesh. Surprisingly the area has had no revolutionary background. It was part of the ancient kingdom of Kalinga where Emperor Ashok fought a bloody battle. Later, when the area was under French sway, the district was the scene of another bloody conflict, the Battle of Bobbili, which is commemorated in a ballad sung by the wandering minstrels.[1] The engagement was so severe that a historian described it as "one of the most ghastly stories which even Indian history has to record." In the post-Independence era, the Communist influence over the area was negligible in the initial stages. In the four elections held in 1952, 1957, 1962 and 1967, the Communists failed to get a single seat from the area and the percentage share of votes polled by them (CPI and CPM combined) was 4.9, 12.7, 5.6 and 4.4 respectively.

The question naturally arises: Why did the Naxalites choose this area and what contributed to their success? Three explanations could be offered. In the first place, the district has a hilly terrain covered by forests which provide ideal conditions for guerilla warfare. Secondly, the Girijans were a terribly discontented lot, subjected as they had been to the most ruthless exploitation by traders and money-lenders from the plains. They were ready to be led by any political party which would espouse their cause. Thirdly, the adjoining Mahendragiri hills of Orissa provided an ideal sanctuary where the rebels could seek shelter in the event of pursuit by the police.

The Girijans or the hill people comprise about 90% of the total population of Srikakulam district. They inhabit what are known as the Agency areas spreading over 509 sq. miles of the Eastern Ghats. The tribals belong mainly to two groups, viz. Jatapu and Savara. Both have their separate languages, but Telugu is generally understood. They lead simple and un-sophisticated lives with little contact with the outside world. Most of them were engaged in agricultural operations while some collected minor forest produce like tamarind which they sold to the merchants from plains at weekly *shandies* (village markets). The British were conscious of the need to protect the Girijans from any exploitation by the plainsmen. As early as 1917, therefore, it was decreed that no land would be transferred from a Girijan to a non-Girijan without the specific permission of the District Collector. The Act was unfortunately observed more in the breach. The traders and money-lenders took full advantage of the grinding poverty of the Girijans. They gave them daily necessities of life like tobacco, kerosene, salt, chilly and cloth on credit and also lent money for the purchase of seeds and payment of taxes. Those unable to clear their debt were made to part with their land. The result was that gradually much of the fertile land was alienated from the Girijans and passed into the hands of plainsmen. The Girijans became hewers of wood and drawers of water in their own country. Some worked as farm servants, some as daily wage earners while some took plots of land on lease.

The landlords squeezed them to the utmost and paid subsistence wages (5 *puttis* per year, one *putti* being about 55 Kgs) to the farm servants and less than half a rupee per day to the daily wage earner.

Those cultivating on lease had to give two-thirds of their produce to the landlord. Their plight was indeed miserable.

It was against this background that Vempatapu Satyanarayana organised the Girijans to fight for their rights. A school teacher from the plains, he had settled in the Agency area. He mobilised the Girijans and forced the landowners and contractors to pay fair wages to them, though this brought him into collision with the vested interests and he had to sacrifice his job in the process. Thereafter Vempatapu Satyanarayana devoted all his time and attention to improving the lot of the Girijans. To establish closer identity with them, he married one woman each from the Jatapu and Savara tribes. Under his leadership, the various issues affecting the Girijans were taken up. These included the right to cultivate waste lands, use of forest produce, increase in the wages of farm servants and daily wage workers, reduction of the landlord's share in lands cultivated on share-cropping basis, reduction of interest on loans, transfer of lands occupied by landlords and *sahukars* to the rightful owners, distribution of consumer goods at fair prices and ending of harassment by the forest, revenue and police officials. The movement achieved a considerable measure of success and, by 1967, a number of demands were conceded. The wages of farm servants rose from 5 *puttis* to 20-25 *puttis*, the landord's share of harvest from lands leased to share croppers was slashed from two-third to one-third, 1500-2000 acres of land were wrested back from the landlords and *sahukars* and more than 5000 acres of waste land came under the possession of Girijans. Apart from these economic gains, the Girijans started becoming politically conscious. Vempatapu Satyanarayana found a good response when he set about forming Girijan Sanghams. These bodies carried out certain functions like settling disputes, managing schools, raising funds, etc. which are normally performed by government officials. Vempatapu Satyanarayana became a very popular figure. The Girijans started calling him "Gappa Guru" or Chief Guru. Some even looked upon him as God.

Panchadi Krishnamurti and C. Tejeswara Rao were the other important leaders of the movement. Subbarao Panigrahi, a famous writer who belonged to Orissa, contributed to extending the Naxalite activities to the bordering villages of Orissa. He stirred the people with his *Jamukula Katha* (a popular folklore form of story-telling) troupe. M.

Appalasuri was another important figure. A significant feature of the movement was the participation of engineering and medical students who provided the middle rank leadership.

The movement was initially confined to fighting for economic demands only. The Naxalbari uprising is said to have opened the eyes of the revolutionary comrades in Srikakulam[2]. Soon after, on October 31, 1967, an incident took place which proved to be a turning point. A large group of tribals marching in a procession to attend a meeting organised by the Marxist Party were intercepted by the landlords at Levidi. A clash ensued. The landlords used their guns and killed two tribals. This inflamed the Girijans and they took a pledge to settle their score. The Girijan movement henceforth became militant.

Vempatapu Satyanarayana organised the Girijans into guerilla squads or *dalams*. At one stage, there were as many as 100 *dalams* consisting of 800 tribesmen.[3] These *dalams* conducted raids on *shandies*, attacked the houses of landlords and money-lenders and looted properties and foodgrains. On March 4, 1968, the Girijans had their first encounter with the police at Pedakarja. The tribals were armed with bows and arrows, spears and muzzle-loaders, but they suffered two casualties due to the superior fire-power of the police. They were, however, not daunted and continued their preparations with meticulous care—selecting hide-outs, giving training in guerilla warfare to the *dalam* members, organising a courier system and collecting whatever arms they could lay their hands on. There was a general realisation that "to meet the armed offensive of the exploiting classes the armed struggle is the only weapon left to them."[4]

It is necessary to clarify at this stage that the Srikakulam leadership, after the split in the Communist Party in 1964, had joined the CPI(M). In 1968 they broke away from the CPI(M) and came under the banner of All India Coordination Committee of Communist Revolutionaries which, in due course, evolved into the CPI(ML). The members of Srikakulam Committee headed by Tejeswara Rao went to Calcutta in October 1968 and met Charu Mazumdar, Kanu Sanyal and Sushital Roy Choudhury. It was decided at the meeting that an insurrection on the pattern of Naxalbari uprising should be organised in Andhra also. The decision was subsequently endorsed on Oct 23, 1968 by the Srikakulam leaders which included Vempatapu Satyanarayana, Panchadi Krishnamurti,

Thamada Ganapati, M. Appalasuri and Tejeswara Rao at Boddapadu, a sleepy village in the plains area of Sompeta *taluk* of Srikakulam. A month later, on November 24, 1968, the Naxalites struck at Garudabhadra. The CPI(ML) regards it as the opening shot of the liberation struggle. A squad of women volunteers preparing for political demonstration was obstructed by the landlord's men, and the women volunteers were manhandled. This aroused the ire of Girijans. About 250 of them belonging to the Sompeta and Tekkali *taluks* collected and forcibly harvested the standing crops of the landlord. The same night Vempatapu Satyanarayana led an attack on the house of a landlord in Pedagottili in Parvathipuram Agency area and looted property worth Rs. 20,000.

The movement from November 25, 1968 onwards was aimed at implementing the following programme:

   a) seizing the property of the landlords;
   b) annihilating the class enemies;
   c) resisting the police; and
   d) building up revolutionary base areas[5].

There were a series of raids at the houses of landlords, moneylenders and their agents in which the Naxalites burnt down their dwellings and looted cash and other property. There were a number of encounters with the police also. It was claimed that during the period from December 20, 1968 to January 30, 1969 no less than 29 policemen, including one circle inspector and one sub-inspector, were killed in action.[6] The special representative of *The Statesman*, in his report of December 14, 1968, mentioned that the state government's writ did not run in scores of isolated mountain hamlets where the tribesmen held complete sway. He also mentioned that the special armed police which had been moved into the area was not able to check the revolt and that the Girijans continued to be in a sullen and un-cooperative attitude.

Charu Mazumdar's visit to Srikakulam in March 1969 gave spurt to the Girijan insurgency. He advised the Srikakulam leaders to concentrate on annihilating the class enemies, building up guerilla squads and starting people's war.[7] It is worthwhile reproducing Charu Mazumdar's experience in a quiet village of Srikakulam in the midst of Girijan rebels:

"Here, in the midst of a jungle surrounded by hills, I am sitting in a room on a hilltop and before me are seated about a score of young men. They are not well known or renowned men, nor men who enjoy an all India fame. But they are men who are young, men who dream. They dream of liberating the tens of crores of peasants who have been exploited and oppressed through the ages, they dream of liberating them from the yoke of exploitation, from the murky depths of ignorance, from grinding poverty, from hunger. They believe in making revolution. It is after a long time that I have attended a meeting like this of Communist revolutionaries where they have taken the vow to sell out their properties and donate the entire sum thus obtained to the Party fund . . . The slogan: 'Let us build Srikakulams in the different areas to support the Srikakulam struggle' instantly changed the atmosphere of the meeting and the very air in the room seemed to have been electrified. All the comrades present resolutely declared that they would build Srikakulams in Telengana, in the districts of the Rayalaseema region, in the whole of Andhra. At that moment, throbbing as it was with the vigorous, bright spirit of revolutionary ardour, one thought repeatedly haunted me—the thought of the heroic revolutionaries of Telengana who lay down their lives fighting. I was thinking that the sacrifice of those glorious fighters has not been in vain; for India's Yenan will be created here."[8]

The Girijan insurgency touched a highwater mark. The Naxalites claimed politcal power over 300 villages of the Agency area. Raids on the houses of landlords and ambushes of police patrols became a regular feature. As a result, many terrified landlords fled from the Agency area and the forest and revenue officials found it difficult to carry out their functions in the Naxalite-infested villages. The rebels set up a Ryotanga Sangram Samithi which was described as the revolutionary mass organisation of the peasants. Violence registered a sharp increase and the Naxalites claimed to have "seized nights from the enemies' hands." Some of these claims may be exaggerated, but it was acknowledged that, "about 100 square miles of mountainous terrain, deep in the interior of Parvathipuram agency, is under the virtual control of the Naxalites," and that "the Andhra Pradesh Government has failed to extend its sway to this 'red area.' "[9]

It is estimated that during 1969 the Naxalites committed 23 murders and 40 dacoities in Srikakulam district.[10] Some of these were particularly gruesome. On the night of May 26, 1969, about 600 Naxalites raided Loharijola village and murdered a landowner, Anguru Induvadana Naidu, in the presence of his wife. One of the Naxalites dipped his hand in the blood of the deceased and made palm impressions at five places on the walls. The Naxalites also ransacked the house and carried away property worth Rs. 12,669. In another incident at Akkupali on June 20, 1969, about 80 armed Naxalites including some women volunteers raided the house of a rich merchant, Bhu Chandra Rao, and killed him notwithstanding desperate pleadings by his wife. According to the widow, the slaying was done by a woman member of the gang, later identified as Panchadi Nirmla.

Here is an account of how a feudal tyrant met his doom:

"On May 11, a landlord named P. Jammu Naidu of Ethamanuguda of Pathapatnam *taluk* was punished to death by 200 people assisted by the guerilla *dalam*. This landlord, who was above fifty, was having seven wives, two of them little girls, and had been committing crimes of every sort. He stepped up his criminal activities especially since March 1968, when the large scale repression was let loose by the police. He grabbed the land and other property of the poor Girijans and some were forced to give their daughters to him as his wives. Not satisfied with his death, the peasants painted slogans with his blood. This demonstrates the intensity of the wrath of the masses against this notorious feudal lord. The brothers of his wives and othe relatives also participated in this action."[11]

The following account of trial of a *sahukar* by the People's Court throws light on the nature of exploitation:

"The *sahukar* (usurer) who is also a merchant, came to the Agency area to collect tamarind from peasants who pay off their loans taken earlier from the *sahukar* by supplying tamarind. The list of borrowers which he brought with him showed that he had lent a total sum of Rs. 280 to peasants of four villages. Against this, he proposed to collect from them 40 *Kavidis* (bundles) of tamarind, which at current market rates, are worth Rs. 1600. That is, the peasants are to pay back nearly 6 rupees for every rupee they borrowed! This had been the normal practice till the revolutionary peasants established their own authority through guerilla struggle. The man was arrested by the peasants and taken to their base area for trial. The man confessed before the people's court that he had been exploiting the peasants and promised never to exploit again. He also promised to obey the rules and regulations of the Samithi and live a just life without exploiting anyone. He begged that one opportunity be given to him for proving his sincerity.

After listening to what he had to say, the people were consulted in order to verify his past record, how he had treated the peasant borrowers, etc. On verification it was found that, compared with other landlords, he had seldom acted brutally. On the basis of this finding and in view of the man's repentant attitude, he was finally set free on the understanding that he would act in accordance with the promise he had made before the people's court."[12]

In sheer brutality, the incident at Bhavanapuram was in a class by itself. On the night of January 18, 1970, eight Naxalites attacked the lonely farm house of Voona Savarayya of Sompeta residing at Bhavanapuram village and stabbed him to death. Thereafter they severed his head and hung it on a bamboo pole erected in front of the house.

Revolutionary songs composed by Satyanarayana and others became popular with the Girijans and fired the imagination of the simple tribals. The following lines were penned by Satyanarayana:

Rise up, oh, ye Adivasi heroes,
And flex the muscles
of your taut and sinewy body
And plunge with the force of a hurricane
Into battle against your class enemies.

Another revolutionary song popular with the Srikakulam Naxalites was in the following refrain:

Awake, oh, tribal hero!
Your sinews are strong as steel.
Lunge forward with the force
    of a tidal wave.
And......
Hurry along, oh worker!
Hurry along, oh peasant!

While the Girijans were in full cry in Srikakulam, the Revolutionary Communist Committee of Andhra Pradesh led by T. Nagi Reddy organised the movement in Warangal, Khammam and Karimnagar districts of Telengana. "A total area covering 5,000 to 6,000 sq. miles and inhabited by about 350,000 to 400,000 population came under the control of the revolutionaries."[13] In April 1969, the Committee adopted 'The Immediate Programme,' which called upon the party workers "to apply the path of people's war to the revolutionary practice in India and to carry it through to the end." They were also directed to mobilise the people and intensify their activities both in the forest as well as the plains areas. T. Nagi Reddy and seven other leaders were however arrested in December 1969. Thereafter Chandra Pulla Reddy took over the leadership of the movement.

The Government soon realised the seriousness of the situation. An inter-state conference of top officials of Andhra Pradesh, Orissa and Madhya Pradesh was held at Visakhapatnam on August 12, 1969 and it was decided to coordinate police action against Naxalites in the bordering areas. Police offensive started in Srikakulam district towards the end of 1969. In the encounters which followed, important Naxalite leaders like Bhaskar Rao, Thamada Ganapathy, Nirmala Krishnamurty, Subbarao Panigrahi and Ramesh Chandra Sahu were killed. These losses greatly upset the Central Organising Committee of the CPI(ML) and it issued a statement in January 1970 calling upon members of the party, "to avenge the dastardly murder of our heroic comrades of Srikakulam by annihilating as many class enemies as possible." It directed the comrades to turn their grief into burning hatred of the class enemy and exhorted them, in Mao's words, to "march ahead along the path crimson with the blood of heroic martyrs." The Srika-kulam comrades were told that losses and setbacks were inevitable in any struggle.

Charu Mazumdar made a desperate attempt to resuscitate the move-ment. In a letter to the Andhra comrades on July 18, 1971[14], Charu Mazumdar stressed the need to form small squads of landless and poor peasants and stated that every such squad should be considered a contingent of the People's Liberation army. The area of operation of the squads should be fixed and area commanders elected from amongst the landless and poor peasants. The petty bourgeois were assigned the role of political commissars. A significant advice contained in the letter was that mass economic work such as land distribution and seizing of harvest should be propagated at various levels by the revolutionary committees, which were further asked to pay attention to the production of foodgrains, etc. This was in sharp contrast to Charu Mazumdar's earlier aversion for economic work. Perhaps it indicated a climb-down on his part in the face of mounting criticism. He went to the extent of conceding that only in this way would mass struggle of the peasantry be linked up with the armed struggle, and the political authority of the party established. Charu Mazumdar ex-pressed his optimism that the Andhra extremists would be able to overcome their weaknesses and their "struggle will develop like an avalanche in the state." However, that was not to be and the movement gradually tapered off in the face of coordinated administrative action.

The shooting down of Vempatapu Satyanarayana and Adibhatla Kailasam, the two top Naxalite leaders of Srikakulam, by the police in an encounter in the Bori Hills of Parvathipuram *taluk* on July 10, 1970 shattered the tribal insurgency in Srikakulam. Both of them were members of the Central Committee of the CPI(ML). While Satyanarayana completely integrated himself with the tribals and or-ganised the *dalams*, Kailasam was the brain behind the movement. However, their death did not signify the end of the Naxalite movement in Andhra Pradesh. As we shall see later, the volcano was to erupt again in the Telengana area with the People's War Group spearheading the movement.

3.2 WEST BENGAL—MIDNAPUR AND BIRBHUM

The greatest of evils and the worst of crimes is poverty.

Bernard Shaw

The Midnapur district of West Bengal bordering Bihar and Orissa witnessed a well planned and well organised Naxalite movement in the Debra and Gopiballavpur Police Station areas. The district has a sizeable tribal population of Santhals, Lodhas and Oraons. The majority of them were landless labourers, though a small proportion owned small plots of land or cultivated the *jotedars'* land under the *barga* system. It was easy for the Communist revolutionaries to work up the land hunger of these simple and unsophisticated *bargadars*. Besides, adept as they were in the use of bows and arrows,they could be deadly if provoked to violence.

Gopiballavpur was selected for its strategic location. It has a long forest infested border with Bihar and Orissa and is linked with the rest of Midnapur only by a bridge over the river Subarnarekha. Debra was an obvious choice because all CPI(M) leaders of the local unit had come out of the party after the Naxalbari uprising and joined the CPI(ML) *en bloc*. From the point of view of terrain, it was unsafe for guerilla action because the area was close to the railway station and lay parallel to the Calcutta-Bombay national highway, besides being dangerously open. But then the hills and forests were adequately substituted by a sympathetic population.

The leading figures of the movement in Debra were Bhabadeb Mondal, an advocate who contested unsuccessfully in the assembly election of 1967 as a CPI(M) candidate and Gunadhar Murmu, a local tribal leader. In Gopiballavpur, the moving spirits were Santosh Rana and

47

Ashim Chatterji. The former was a first class MSc(Tech) from Calcutta University; the latter a product of the Presidency College, Calcutta.

After the Naxalbari uprising in 1967, a section of CPI(M) workers in Midnapur started propagating the extremist line. They supported the *kisans* and *bargadars* during the harvest in 1967 and worked up a movement against the *jotedars*. Santosh Rana took the job of a teacher in Nayabasan H S School, PS Gopiballavpur and started political work. He addressed meetings of landless *kisans*, especially Santhals, and incited them to rise in revolt against the capitalist *jotedars*, seize their *benami* and vested lands and even loot paddy from the granaries. Ashim Chatterji and a host of other students from Calcutta also carried out propaganda on similar lines. A remarkable feature of the movement was that the Calcutta bravos completely identified themselves with the underdogs. No doubt, some of them were not able to withstand the rigours of rural life, but those who stayed on merged themselves into the background. They lived with the tribals, worked with them in the fields, ate the same food and shared their weal and woe in general. They gave their wages to the needy and arranged to distribute medicines among the sick. This made them immensely popular and they moved in the countryside like fish in water.

In Debra, the movement started on economic issues: there were demonstrations against hoarders and black-marketeers and demands to raise the wages of agricultural labourers. But in due course, the peasants' struggle against the *jotedars* "began to overstep the pale of economic demands;[1] seizure of power through armed struggle was presented as a distinct possibility. The CPI(M) did not approve of this political twist to the movement and expelled Bhabadeb Mondal and Gunadhar Murmu from the party. But the idea had caught on and there was no stopping it. The success achieved by the Naxalite guerillas in Srikakulam and Mushahari enthused the party workers in Debra. The beginnings of the struggle in Gopiballavpur further boosted their revolutionary fervour.

The movement in Debra-Gopiballavpur showed a tactical improvement over the Naxalbari uprising.[2] In Naxalbari, trouble had started with the share-croppers lifting stocks of paddy and seizing plots of land. The movement had not turned violent for about two months. In Midnapur, occupation of land was given secondary importance.

48

The perspective placed before the party workers was capture of power through an armed struggle, the main strand of which was to be annihilation of class enemies. The CPI(ML) therefore organised a series of raids on the houses of *jotedars* and money-lenders. It was the same story all over with difference of shade only. The class enemies were killed, their property and arms looted, stocks of foodgrains distributed among the poor and landless peasants, and the deeds and documents burnt. This tactical variation, it was said, represented a higher stage of struggle—that of guerilla warfare.

The movement in Gopiballavpur was launched in August 1969. In a major action on September 27, 1969, the Naxalites led by Santosh Rana attacked the house of a *jotedar*, Nagen Senapati, assaulted him and his brother and snatched away a gun. Nagen Senapati sustained serious injuries but his brother succumbed. On October 16, a *jotedar* of village Chowbazar was killed by Naxalites led by Mihir Rana, brother of Santosh Rana. Altogether 12 big landholders were killed during October-November in the Gopiballavpur area[3]. In Debra, the movement started with a bang on October 1, 1969. About 1000 adivasis, *kisans* and *khet mazdoors* led by Gunadhar Murmu came in a procession and gheraoed the house of Kanai Kuity of village Saldahari. The mob was armed with *lathis*, bows and arrows, *tangis* and spears. The *jotedar* managed to escape but the extremists ransacked his house. All deeds pertaining to land transactions were destroyed by burning. On October 4, the Naxalites attacked the house of Pulin Mondal of village Bhuyabasa and looted Rs. 10,000 in cash, apart from other items. On October 13, the guerillas annihilated *jotedar* Jiban Das of village Hatberia. Another *jotedar*, Dwija Ray of village Dua was liquidated on October 18. Satish Paria of village Mukundapur, a *jotedar* who had actively helped the police, was killed on October 23.

A number of *jotedars*, rich peasants and big businessmen of Debra took shelter in Midnapur town. There was great panic, particularly after Gunadhar Murmu, the Santhal guerila leader, issued a *gira* after the traditional tribal custom by tying a knot of the bark of a sal tree, symbolising revenge, and called upon his followers to take severe action against the *jotedars* and the district officials. The authorities were greatly concerned. *The Statseman* correspondent reported on December 2 that the West Bengal Government had decided to launch an "all-out attack" on the Naxalites in Debra along with police action already being carried out in Gopiballavpur. Quoting authoritative sources, the correspondent added that the police had been asked to "shoot to kill," if necessary. Three more companies of armed police, including one company of the Eastern Frontier Rifles, were moved into Debra and Gopiballavpur areas. In the operations which followed, about 300 extremists were arrested[4], but it is significant that the top leadership comprising Santosh Rana, Ashim Chatterji, Bhabadeb Mondal and Gunadhar Murmu eluded the police dragnet for quite some time. This was possible because they had been able to build a fairly sound underground apparatus. The following write-up in the *Ananda Bazar Patrika* of December 2, 1969 by a correspondent who visited the Debra-Gopiballavpur areas is revealing:

"But one thing is clear; so far hardly anyone has come forward to cooperate with the police. The reason, according to the police, is fear of the Naxalites. It is difficult to ascertain whether it is because of fear or for love for the Naxalites. The fact, however, remains that the police have so far been unable to capture their leaders. Everyone knows that almost all the leaders are still here in this area, yet no one gets any information about them. This means that no one is giving the information and so the leaders are still able to live underground.

In spite of the presence of and patrolling by the police, the majority of the local well-to-do people prefer to maintain good terms with the Naxalites.The police explain away this sort of affair by stating that the people still have fears of the Naxalites. But the Naxalites point to this fact as a proof of their claim that they continue to wield strong influence in the area. Everyone knows, they claim, that the police are quite unable to protect them (the well-to-do). The local people also admit that there are quite a few villages in Debra where the police dare not enter in small numbers—two or three men—even when armed with rifles. They dare to enter into those places only when they are twenty or more in number and armed with rifles. And in Gopiballavpur there are no less than three hundred such villages."

The annihilation campaign continued till early 1970. It is said that the CPI(ML)'s call to avenge the death of Srikakulam martyrs and Charu Mazumdar's call to "spread the struggle in waves" provided the necessary impetus. In Gopiballavpur, Ashu Mahapatra, a *jotedar* whom the Naxalites described as a "vulture of a man" was killed on March 5. Within two days, the guerillas carried out another raid on March 7 at the house of *jotedar* Kedar Ghose and murdered his son. Another *jotedar*, Narayan Pati, who was accused of "building up a counter revolutionary force of hired goondas," was liquidated on March 21. In Debra, the peasant guerillas annihilated Kanai Kuiti, who had earlier escaped an attempt on his life, on March 19. Kuiti was alleged to be "an embodiment of ruthless feudal domination in the countryside." In another action on March 22, Hafizuddin Mallik, a *jotedar* and a usurer, was beheaded while returning from the market.

West Bengal was then under a United Front Government in which Sri Jyoti Basu, CPI(M) leader, held charge of the police portfolio. It has been said that for "understandable reasons" the Home Minister was unwilling to do everything possible to put down the revolt and that the police action did not go beyond containing the activities of the Naxalites and throwing a cordon around the affected villages.[5] But after the fall of the United Front Government in March 1970 and the imposition of President's Rule in the State, the police force marched into the area in strength and snuffed out the movement.

Birbhum district also witnessed intense Naxalite violence. It had a predominantly agricultural economy which was not able to absorb the educated youth, a large number of whom were unemployed. There was no charismatic leader in the district and I was surprised to find during my visit to the area in the second half of July 1971 that the groundwork had been done by little known students. Sudev Biswas, B.E (Metallurgy) had done pioneering work in disseminating Charu Mazumdar's gospel among the urban youth. Kshitish Chatterjee, M.Sc and Biren Ghosh, B.Sc also put in hard work to indoctrinate the younger elements. Birbhum was till then one of the quiet districts of West Bengal. Naxalite activities started about the middle of 1970, when wall slogans appeared in Suri, Rampurhat and at other places. This was followed by burning of schools, colleges and government offices in July 1970. The first killing of a class enemy took place in December

1970. Naxalite activities thereafter were on a high trajectory till the middle of 1971. Month-wise, the violent incidents were: January-44, February-90, March-116, April-119, May-70 and June-100. The police stations worst affected were Suri, Rampurhat and Bolpur. The total strength of CPI(ML) activists in the district was about 400, the bulk of them being drawn from amongst the urban educated youth.

Birbhum witnessed the largest number of arms-snatching incidents. The first such incident took place on February 8, 1971. Month-wise, the figures till the middle of 1971 were: February-3, March-11, April-64, May-42 and June-41. The weapons snatched were from policemen and also from private licencees, most of whom surrendered their weapons without any resistance.

The government was alarmed at these developments and combined army-police operations were undertaken in Birbhum district from July onwards. Units of the 4th Rajput Infantry Battalion, CRPF(5 Coys), State Armed Police (2 Coys), Eastern Frontier Rifles (2 Platoons), National Volunteer Force (2 Coys) and Saurashtra Reserve Police (2 Coys) were deployed. The Rajput Battalion was mostly utilised for combing operations. The CRP, apart from assisting in raids, guarded the jail, State Bank and some colleges. The SAP was deployed in the Vishwabharati campus. The EFR units were deployed in Nalhati and Rajnagar. The NVF guarded government buildings and residences of senior officers. The SRP Coys were utilised for raids and other law and order duties. The operations had the desired effect. About 150 CPI(ML) activists were arrested, the remaining having fled to the adjoining districts of Burdwan, Murshidabad and Santhal Parganas. The results of the operations were not commensurate with the level of force mobilised for the purpose. This was partly due to the absence of precise intelligence and partly due to the premature publicity given to the operations in the media. Nevertheless the movement in Birbhum virtually collapsed after the action of the security forces.

The Naxalite influence extended to other districts of West Bengal also. Calcutta was the nerve-centre. The CPI(ML), besides, had sizeable following in 24 Parganas, Hooghly, Howrah, Burdwan, Malda, Nadia, Jalpaiguri and Darjeeling districts.

The non-CPI(ML) groups active in the State included the Committee of Communist Revolutionaries, which had following in Howrah and parts of 24 Parganas and Darjeeling, the Parimal Das Gupta group which was strong among the industrial labour in Calcutta, the Abad group, the Puber Hawa group and the Revolutionary Communist Council of India, whose following was limited to Calcutta.

3.3   BIHAR AND UTTAR PRADESH

The sickle that once reaped the golden corn
Today shall reap the venomous heads that peasants
scorn.

—Satchithanandanan

The Mushahari block in Muzaffarpur district of Bihar and the Palia area in Lakhimpur-Kheri district of UP emerged as two strong pockets of Naxalite influence in these states.

Bihar

The Mushahari block of Muzaffarpur district in Bihar witnessed stirrings on the Naxalbari pattern. It covered twelve villages with a population of about 10,000 people. There were disputes between landlords and peasantry over occupancy rights, cutting of trees, etc and, besides, the peasantry nursed the grievance of being subjected to various forms of social oppression by the upper classes. It was an explosive mixture, and the sparks flying off from Naxalbari set it ablaze.

In the early stages, Naxalite activities in the area were confined to two or three villages with Gangapur as the centre. In April 1968, the peasants of Gangapur harvested the *arahar* (a kind of pulse) crop of the landlord in broad daylight. This was the starting point of trouble. Retaliation was quick. Bijli Singh, the *zamindar* of Narsinghpur, organised an attack on the peasants with 300 men armed with *lathis*, spears, swords, daggers and firearms. The landlord himself came on an elephant and brought two cartloads of stones.[1] A bizarre fight followed and it went on for about four hours. The landlord and his hoodlums eventually took to their heels. "The humbling of this very powerful landlord by the poor peasantry, mostly belonging to scheduled castes (Harijans) had a magic effect on the neighbouring villages. The landlords grew panicky and the peasants became further courageous and far more determined. Now they felt that the landlords could be beaten and driven out if the peasants were united."[2] Gangapur became a symbol of the fighting peasantry and the Mushahari struggle took a "qualitative leap." Soon after, Kisan Sangram Samitis (Peasants' Action Committees) and Gram Rakshak Dals (Village Defence Squads) were organised in most of the villages. The Dals were instructed to (i) annihilate the landlords and their *goondas,* (ii) seize forcibly the properties of the rich people and (iii) establish people's rule in the villages[3].

In August 1968, the peasants of Harkesh village seized some land. The landlord sought police help and got one peasant arrested. As the news spread, peasants of the entire village and from nearby places gathered, got the arrested peasant released and beat up the landlord. Class solidarity had taken shape. It is said that the village remained disturbed for about three days. The government thereupon set up a police camp in the area under the charge of a Deputy Superintendent of Police with arrangements for patrolling by armed police in the interior villages. Satyanaryan Singh, the Naxalite leader, alleges that this was followed by "massive police repression" in the course of which peasants were assaulted, arrested, their huts burnt and properties plundered. The Naxalite leaders went underground. This took the movement to the second stage—the stage of armed guerilla struggle.

In the second phase, a clash took place in village Lakhanuari, P.S. Paru in April 1969. The landless peasants had forcibly harvested the crop on 14 acres of land belonging to a landlord. The landlord's men replied with guns and other lethal weapons. The Naxalite guerillas fought back and killed one of the landlord's retainers. A second attack was made in village Paharchar, PS Baruraj in June 1969. The Naxalites murdered the landlord and his two accomplices, seized all the deeds and documents concerning land and confiscated the ornaments pawned by the poor peasants. Hundreds of peasants gathered at Paharchar after the raid and, in their presence, all the deeds and documents were burnt and the ornaments returned to their legitimate owners. Then came the most impressive attack on the landlord of Narsinghpur. On the night of July 5, 1969, the Communist revolutionaries raided the house of Bijli Singh. Three class enemies were annihilated and property worth Rs. 20,000 was looted. Yet another daring attack took place in Baradaud village, PS Paru in August 1969. Kalika Singh, a landlord who had helped the police in tracing underground revolutionaries, was annihilated while taking tea in a road-side shop.

These chain of incidents alarmed the authorities, and senior officers of the police and magistracy visited the area. The Adviser to the Governor held a conference of all the Deputy Commissioners and Superintendents of Police of Tirhut Division to review the situation. It was decided to undertake extensive combing operations to track down the Naxalites. The movement in Mushahari thereafter gradually lost its momentum.

There is reason to believe that Mushahari Naxalites were assisted by comrades from West Bengal in their struggle. Confessions made by some arrested persons of the Mushahari block disclosed that party cadres from West Bengal had infiltrated into North Bihar and given training to kindred spirits in the art of making bombs.

The Mushahari struggle caused ripples in other parts of Bihar also. It was claimed that the entire North Bihar had been, "shaken out of its *samadhi* (trance)." The contiguous districts of Darbhanga and Champaran particularly felt the impact. The extremists incited the *adivasis* of Chhota Nagpur also. The Bihar State Coordination Committee, in June 1968, called upon the *adivasis* to (i) unleash revolutionary struggles against the landlords, *sahukars* and their agents, (ii) form village committees and establish 'People's Raj', (iii) unite with the other revolutionary classes, especially the militant working class, and (iv) expose and eliminate the disruptors, opportunists and careerists from their ranks. The *adivasis* were exhorted to fight the way, "the Great Birsa, the Great Siddu and Kanu fought against the foreign and native oppressors."[4]

The Naxalite activities in Chhota Nagpur[5] area first came into limelight in May 1970 when 54 men belonging to the MMG group (Man, Money and Gun) were arrested from the forests of Jaduguda following a massive police operation. Most of them were Bengalis. But what really made the incident sensational was the presence of a British blonde, Miss Mary Tyler, among them. Later, she wrote poignantly that the Naxalites' crime was

"...the crime of all those who cannot remain unmoved and inactive in an India where a child crawls in the dust with a begging bowl; where a poor girl can be sold as a rich man's plaything; where an old woman must half-starve herself in order to buy social acceptance from the powers that be in her village; where countless people die of sheer neglect; where many are hungry while food is hoarded for profit; where usurers and tricksters extort the fruits of labour from those who do the work; where the honest suffer whilst the villainous prosper; where justice is the exception and injustice the rule; and where the total physical and mental energy of millions of people is spent on the struggle for mere survival."[6]

The leader of the MMG, Subroto Roy, attributed the failure of the group to their lack of adequate knowledge of topography of the area and their physical inability to negotiate the rugged terrain of forests and hills.

The Naxalite violence which erupted in Singhbhum and Ranchi districts had more serious dimensions. Jamshedpur became a mini-Calcutta and there were instances of attacks on educational institutions, government offices and police pickets. The first annihilation took place on September 20, 1970, when a member of Tata Town Security Department, who was alleged to be a police informer, was killed. In October, a TELCO worker said to be a CPI supporter, and in November a TISCO Security Guard were stabbed to death. Next month, a TELCO employee met the same fate and a TISCO security guard sustained bomb injuries when the Naxalites attacked a local school. A few days later, a businessman was done to death.

The first attack on educational institutions in Jamshedpur took place on August 1, 1970. Thereafter several secondary and higher secondary schools in the town were raided. There were raids on clubs and bars also, the main meeting centres of the bourgeoisie. In January 1971, four buses belonging to the State Transport Corporation were burnt by the Naxalites. The same month, a Pushpak aircraft belonging to the Jamshedpur Flying Club was also bombed and destroyed. Police patrol parties were not spared and there were abortive attempts to kill individual police officers. In the rural areas of Singhbhum district, the Naxalites were active mostly in the region bordering Gopiballavpur of West Bengal. A police sub-inspector's house in Kharswan was attacked in September 1970 and bombs were thrown at the house of a mine manager in the same area.

Ranchi also witnessed Naxalite activities on a fairly big scale. There were four main areas where they were active: Kolebira in Simdega sub-division; Mandar, Burmu and Khelari on the Palamau-Hazaribagh border; Silli on the Ranchi-Purulia road and Ranchi town itself. In Ranchi town, the Naxalites threw crackers at the local Jana Sangh office on September 1, 1970. They also raided the local branch of the British Council Library.

In Dhanbad district, the Naxalites were active mostly among the students. In November 1970, a statue of Mahatma Gandhi was demolished in the town. In the following month, there was an unsuccessful attempt to damage the micro-wave relay station on the outskirts of the town. In January 1971, the office of the Life Insurance Corporation at Sindri was raided.

Uttar Pradesh

The Palia area is a part of the Lakhimpur district in Uttar Pradesh and is situated in its northern Terai region. The area was fully covered with dense forests and inhabited by tribals called the Tharus. Later, the State Government encouraged poor peasants from other areas, especially eastern UP, to come to Palia, clear the forests and undertake cultivation. They were given the inducement of owning 10-12 acres of land. In actual fact, however, the landlords and other influential men forcibly occupied big chunks of land and ejected the poor peasants, depriving them of the benefit of their hard work. This provided the Naxalites with a fertile ground for agitation, and it was claimed that "just after Naxalbari the whole of this Terai region resounded with the call of the peasants' struggle for land."[7] Actually, however, the movement was confined to eleven villages at the beginning, though in due course it spread to about 30 villages.

The party's avowed objective was to clear the area of big farmers, *goondas*, corrupt political leaders and moneylenders, all of whom were declared "enemies." The "friends" included all the poor people, whether they were Tharus, Rai Sikhs, original residents of the district or people from the eastern districts. The settlers having legal rights over their plots of land ranging from 10 to 20 acres were looked upon as "allies." Led by Vishwanath Tewari, the extremists were responsible for a number of incidents. In a raid in village Bhanpuri Khajuria in February 1969, the extremists decamped with three firearms including a pistol, a revolver and a DBBL gun. On April 2, 1969, the extremists raided the houses of two residents of village Raninagar and looted property worth Rs. 850, besides taking away an SBBL gun. The then Chief Minister of Uttar Pradesh, Sri C B Gupta, admitted on May 8, 1969, that Naxalites were active in parts of the State, and attributed their activities to the irregularities, wrongs and injustices committed by some village *pradhans* in the distribution of *gaon sabha* land. "Congressmen, non-Congressmen and even law-makers have been parties to this wrong distribution of land.[8] On August 19, 1969, replying to a question in the Vidhan Sabha, the Chief Minister said that adequate police arrangements had been made in Lakhimpur district to curb the activities of lawless elements and a special squad of the PAC posted in the area.

The Naxalites of Palia area received help and shelter from peasants across the border in Nepal. Most of these peasants were from the eastern districts of UP and were facing the threat of being driven out of Nepal. Willy-nilly they felt that they could survive in Nepal only with the help of the Naxalites. The Naxalites, on the other hand, found them good patrons.

The Naxalite movement in Palia never assumed the proportions which could justify the publicity it received.[9] The party organisation in the area was essentially weak. The CPI(ML) mouthpiece *Liberation* of April 1969 itself stated that in the intial stages the Palia unit consisted of only 12 regular members, "only three of whom were ready to take up arms and the rest were at best sympathisers." Their preparations were inadequate and they did not have a well-defined programme. Revolutionary peasant committees were set up in three villages but they hardly functioned. The party admitted having suffered "severe losses" in 1970. These were attributed to failure to organise squads of poor and landless peasants at the village level, excessive reliance on firearms and neglect of conventional weapons, failure to rouse the people for class struggle through annihilation of class enemies, and individualism, commandism and other petty bourgeois tendencies in some of the leaders.[10]

With all its weakness and shortcomings, the movement in Palia had two distinguishing features. One, while concentrating on the problem of land, it did not neglect the other economic issues. It directed the peasants to stop payment of a share of the produce to landlords and big farmers and also payments of old debts to the moneylenders. Two, it realised the importance of mass organisation in developing peasant struggles. The party deplored having under-estimated this aspect in the early stages of the movement. "We could not fully assimilate the teachings of Comrade Mao and thought that the 'rural base area of peasant struggle' could be built up only by a handful of revolutionaries sitting in the forest. Several months passed before we again cared to study the 'Mass Line' of Chairman Mao and began to go to the people. The mass line is being assimilated by us only gradually during the course of our struggle."[11]

Apart from Lakhimpur Kheri, stray incidents of violence occurred in Kanpur, Unnao, Hardoi, Farrukhabad, Bareilly, Moradabad, Baharaich, Varanasi and Azamgarh. The entire State was divided into two zones by the CPI(ML) for organisational purposes, the Eastern Zone and the Western Zone. The former was placed under Shiv Kumar Mishra and the latter under Mahendra Singh, both Central Committee members. Shiv Kumar Singh's arrest in November 1970 was a severe jolt to the party. Thereafter the Naxalite activities were largely in the nature of propaganda work involving distribution of pamphlets and leaflets, writing slogans and holding of study classes. The party also brought out a journal called *Mukti Path* to propagate its ideology.

Bihar and UP together account for about one-third of the total rural poor of the country. The economic problems and the exacerbating social tensions in these two states hold very ominous portents for the future.

3.4   OTHER STATES

The seed ye sow, another reaps;
The wealth ye find, another keeps;
The robes ye weave, another wears;
The arms ye forge, another bears.
                                        —Shelley

The Naxalite activities spread far and wide. Large parts of the country were affected.

In Orissa, the districts particularly affected were Koraput and Ganjam on Andhra border and Mayurbhanj on West Bengal border. Actually the activities in these areas were a spill-over of Naxalite activities in the bordering Srikakulam district of Andhra Pradesh and Midnapur district of West Bengal.The extremists formed a State Coordination Committee on March 14, 1968 with D.B.M. Patnaik as Convener; the other members of the Committee were Jaladhar Nanda, Rabi Das, Kundan Ram, Nagabhushanam Patnaik, Dinabandhu Samal and Jagannath Misra. It was, however, dissolved in 1969 at the behest of Charu Mazumdar and the different regions of the State were attached to the extremist organisations of the neighbouring states. Thus Koraput and Ganjam districts of south Orissa were tagged on to Srikakulam Regional Committee, while Mayurbhanj and Balasore districts of north Orissa were linked to the Coordination Committee of West Bengal. Sambalpur and Sundergarh districts in north-west Orissa were attached to the South Bihar Committee. These committees instigated the tribals to commit various acts of violence. They also held classes, distributed leaflets and organised arms training. The State Government took cognizance of their activities and instituted the Gunupur Conspiracy Case against 71 extremists out of which 51 were charge-sheeted. The arrest of Naxalite leaders caused setback to the movement in south Orissa. In the northern parts, the first violent incident happened on February 26, 1971, when the extremists killed a school teacher and a Gram Rakshi.

On June 5, 1971, they attacked a police post at Bholla, stabbed the Havildar and set fire to the police van. Here also the activities suffered setback after the arrests of Ashim Chatterjee and Santosh Rana. The peculiar features of the Naxalite movement in Orissa were that it was confined to the tribal areas while the coastal districts which are politically more conscious remained comparatively free, and that the State leaders generally played second fiddle to the Naxalite leaders of either Andhra Pradesh or West Bengal.

In Madhya Pradesh, the districts in the Chhatisgarh region, namely Raipur, Durg, Bastar, Bilaspur, Sarguja and Raigarh were affected. A number of party cells were formed in these districts under the guidance of Jogu Roy, the most important CPI(ML) leader of the region. A Krantikari Kisan Mazdoor Party was also constituted. It had some following in Bhopal, Gwalior and Ujjain districts. The *adivasis* in Bastar were particularly receptive to Naxalite propaganda as they nursed a feeling of neglect by the state government. Naxalite posters appeared in Jagdalpur, the district headquarters.

In the Punjab, the Naxalite activities were particularly noticed in Jalandhar, Ludhiana and Sangrur districts. The Naxalites committed terrorist acts involving murder of landlords, moneylenders, farmers and policemen.They even had the audacity to kill a Deputy Superintendent of Police and ransack firearms from a police post in Sangrur district in September 1971. They showed hostility to the rightist elements also; the State Secretary of Swatantra Party, Basant Singh, was annihilated. There was, besides, a planned effort to spread Naxalite ideology among the students and youth with particular focus on those from the backward classes and tribal groups. Revolutionary writers were active in the State and they produced prolific amount of Naxalite literature. The important journals were *People's Path* in English and *Lok Yudh*, *Bagawat* and *Lakeer* in Punjabi. The Punjab Naxalites also made an attempt to forge links with their counterparts in Himachal Pradesh and made frequent visits to that State. Some hide-outs were established in the Garhshankar *tehsil* of Hoshiarpur district bordering Kangra to facilitate contacts between the Naxalites of the two states. The Naxalite activities in the Punjab however suffered due to two reasons: the police pressure which led to the liquidation of leading cadres, and intense factionalism within the party with one group owing allegiance to J.S. Sohal and the other following Baburam Vairagi. The efforts of Baba Gurmukh Singh, who provided guidance and inspiration to the Naxalites of the State, to patch up their differences did not yield any substantial results.

In Jammu & Kashmir, the Democratic Conference, an affiliate of the CPI(ML), was split into two distinct groups, the Saraf group and the Sethi group. The Sethi group did not agree with the programme of annihilation of class enemies nor did it endorse the slogan 'China's Chairman is our Chairman, China's path is our path'.The Saraf group, on the other hand, fully believed in armed actions and favoured launching of people's war on the Chinese pattern. Ram Piara Saraf was a member of the Polit Bureau and also of the Central Committee of the CPI(ML). He was apprehended by the police on March 2, 1971. The documents recovered from his possession showed that he was functioning as Organiser of the Northern Region comprising UP, Punjab, Haryana, J&K and Delhi. I had occasion to meet him on March 6,1971. He was totally commited to the Naxalite ideology and firmly believed that class struggle was unavoidable under the existing conditions. Just as 'action' and ' reaction' explained a mechanism and 'plus' and 'minus' were behind all calculations of mathematics, similarly contradictions leading to class struggle were an integral part of the social system, Saraf explained. His interpretations of the *Ramayana* and *Mahabharata* to justify the resort to violence was amazing. He said that even Lord Rama had to wage a battle to defeat Ravana and that in *Mahabharata* the Pandavas had to fight for their land with the Kauravas.

In Rajasthan, the Naxalites were scattered in the districts of Ganganagar, Sikar, Chittorgarh and Jaipur. They functioned independently and there was no state level coordination in their activities.

In Maharashtra, the appearance of pro-Mao slogans in Bombay and hand-written posters hailing Miss Ajitha Narayanan, a suspect in Kerala police station attacks, were the only manifestations of Naxalite activity.

In Kerala, there were different shades of Naxalism. The CPI(ML) presence was felt mainly in Cannannore (Kannur) and Calicut (Kozhikode) districts of Malabar, and in Kottayam, Quilon (Kollam) and Trivandrum (Thiruvananthapuram) districts. Ambady Sankarankutty Menon, Secretary of the Party, was however arrested on October 10,

1970 and this demoralised the party cadres. The State Committee was thereupon reconstituted with K.P. Gopalan as its Secretary. He implemented the policy of annihilation of class enemies and there were four violent incidents in Trivandrum and Quilon districts on Nov 14-15, 1970. The police arrested the accused and thereafter the activities of the group were on a low key. The other important group was Communist Revolutionary Party led by K.P.R. Gopalan. This faction, while subscribing to the theory of armed revolution, was at the same time in favour of exploiting the parliamentary forum to propagate its ideology. It therefore fielded candidates in the mid-term election to the State Assembly; but all of them lost their deposits. The Worker's Revolutionary Party led by A. Achuthan was avowedly militant. It had a small following in Trivandrum, Ernakulam and Alleppey (Alappuzha) districts. The fourth significant group was that of Kunnikkal Narayanan. It hit the headlines when members of the group attacked the Tellicherry and Pulppalli police stations in 1968. The subsequent apprehension of Kunnikkal Narayanan caused setback to the group.

In Tamil Nadu, public and official attention to Naxalite activities was drawn for the first time by an accidental explosion of a country bomb which was being clandestinely manufactured in Pennadam village, South Arcot district in February 1970. Three persons including a student of Annamalai University were killed as a consequence. The Naxalite activities were otherwise confined to display of posters in some districts and providing shelter to extremists from Kerala and Andhra Pradesh.

In Assam, the extremist activities were limited to circulation of posters and leaflets in Goalpara, Kamrup, Darrang, Nowgong, Sibsagar, Lakhimpur and Cachar districts. The arrest of some Naxalites revealed that they had received training in the use of explosives in rebel Naga camps in Nagaland; manuals seized from their possession contained instructions on sabotage activities. In Tripura, the Naxalite groups were able to set up cells for students and youth, and there were a number of incidents involving raids on educational institutions in Agartala.

In Delhi, the Naxalite ideology attracted many students of the University campus. The institutions particularly affected were the St. Stephen's College and the Delhi School of Economics. The total number of Naxalites was around 50 only but they had a large group of vocal and silent supporters and admirers among the student community. The girls were not to be left behind and there were small groups of Marxist-Leninists in Indraprastha College, Miranda House and Lady Sri Ram College. It has been said that some of them were drawn to the ideology because their boy friends were Naxalites. Delhi University had a well identified group of students and teachers who had pronounced leftist inclinations. They openly talked of violent methods for restructuring the society and initiating reforms. Such ideas were freely debated in the associations and clubs. One such politico-cultural club known as 'Yugantak' particularly caught the imagination of the young for its open advocacy of revolution. It staged many plays in the campus and outside. A powerful case for revolution was made in a play called *India 1969* staged in Miranda House and Tagore Hall. In what appeared to be a real life denouement of the play, the Stephenians who had acted disappeared in 1970 to work for the revolution they had talked of from the stage. About 20 students were found missing from the University campus and were reported to have gone to West Bengal, Bihar and Assam to work among the poor and landless peasants. It is interesting that most of them came from the higher strata of society. Three of them were the sons of ICS Officers, one was the son of an academician and the others were wards of senior government officers. It would however appear that these students were attracted more by the romance of Naxalite philosophy. They were not able to stand the rigours of village life and, in due course, the 'mod' Naxalites returned to their hearths.

4

THE BLAZE

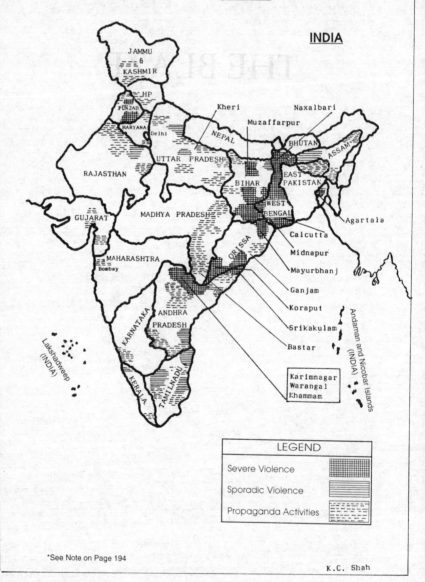

AREAS AFFECTED BY NAXALITE ACTIVITIES
(1970-71)

INDIA

JAMMU & KASHMIR

HP

PUNJAB

HARYANA

Delhi

Kheri

Muzaffarpur

Naxalbari

NEPAL

BHUTAN

ASSAM

RAJASTHAN

UTTAR PRADESH

BIHAR

EAST PAKISTAN

GUJARAT

MADHYA PRADESH

WEST BENGAL

Agartala

ORISSA

Calcutta

Midnapur

Mayurbhanj

Ganjam

Koraput

Srikakulam

Bastar

MAHARASHTRA

Bombay

KARNATAKA

ANDHRA PRADESH

Andaman and Nicobar Islands (INDIA)

Lakshadweep (INDIA)

KERALA

TAMILNADU

Karimnagar
Warangal
Khammam

LEGEND	
Severe Violence	
Sporadic Violence	
Propaganda Activities	

*See Note on Page 194

K.C. Shah

4   THE BLAZE

If the country does not belong to everyone it
will belong to no one.

—Tupamaro Manifesto

The Naxalite violence was at a peak from about the middle of 1970 to the middle of 1971. Naxalism became a major component in the country's political life. Terrorist violence in different states produced a tremendous impact. The political parties realised the emergence of a new force, the government became conscious of a new threat not only to law and order but to the very existence of the democratic set up in the country, and the people in general either looked forward expectantly or were gripped with a sense of fear depending upon the class they came from or the interests they upheld.

Decade of Liberation

The spurt in Naxalite activities is to be attributed mainly to three reasons. Firstly, the Naxalite leaders made frenzied exhortations to the rank and file to step up the tempo of the movement and spread armed struggle to every nook and corner of the country. Satyanaryan Singh, the Naxalite leader of Bihar, exhorted the people to "create hundreds of Naxalbaris throughout the length and breadth of the country. The urgency of the task was underscored by the fantastic argument that India's ruling classes were making war preparations to suit the global strategy of US imperialism and Soviet social imperialism and that they were hatching plans of war against China. It was stressed that their unleashing of revolutionary people's war throughout the country would frustrate the imperialist plot of using India as a base for aggression against China. Charu Mazumdar's slogan 'China's Chairman is our Chairman, China's Path is Our path' gained wide currency during this period. Charu's assessment was that "every corner of India is like a volcano" about to erupt and he predicted "a mightly storm of revolution by 1971". He even set the target for the liberation of India by 1975. How facile his reasoning was would be clear from the following paragraph:

> "When I say 'Make the 70s the Decade of Liberation' I cannot think beyond 1975. The idea of today's armed struggle was first born in the mind of one man. That idea has now filled the minds of ten million people. If the new revolutionary consciousness, born only in 1967, can permeate the minds of 10 million people in 1970, why is it impossible then for those 10 millions to rouse and mobilize the 500 million people of India in a surging people's war by 1975?"[1]

Brave words! But certainly not sound logic. In any case, this clarion call captured the imagination of large segments of party workers.

Secondly, Charu Mazumdar's call to the students and youth in March 1970 to plunge into the revolutionary struggle "here and now" was responded to by sizeable sections of the West Bengal youth. Charu drew inspiration from China, said that the students and youth there had given up their studies at the time of Cultural Revolution, and advised the students in the country not to waste their energy in passing examinations. In words which invariably had the ring of battle-cry, he called upon the students to have faith in Mao Tse-tung Thought which was "smashing the old world and building a new world", and in the Communist Party of India (Marxist-Leninist) which could "never take the wrong road". The students and youth were advised to integrate themselves with the poor and landless peasants and go to the villages in large numbers.

> "Form small squads of students of the schools and colleges in your locality. Each squad should have 4 or 5 students. Then make your programmes for going to the villages even when you have short holidays of only 4 or 5 days. No squad should be formed with girls alone. This is because girls would need some kind of shelter for spending the night. Each of you should take with him a copy of the *Quotations From Chairman Mao Tse-tung*. Take as little money with you as possible and other articles in a kit-bag. Once you go to the

village you are not to seek comforts and good food or shelter. Rather you should compete with one another in enduring hardships. You should not stop and stay at any one place other than for spending the night. You should always be on the move and go from one village to another walking fifteen miles a day on the average. During the journey make acquaintance only with the poor and landless peasants, learn from them, read out quotations of Chairman Mao to them and acquaint them with Mao Tse-tung Thought as much as you can. Tell them of the heroic exploits of the revolutionary peasant war that is now raging in India."[2]

The students and youth were also advised to form Red Guard squads in their schools and colleges and in their respective localities. Every squad was to be led by a comander and have a well-defined jurisdiction. "The Red Guards of today", it was said, "will become later fighters of the People's Liberation Army (PLA) of India".

Thirdly, the working class, "the most revolutionary class and the most organised detachment of the Indian people" was urged to rally under the leadership of the CPI(ML) and march forward along the path of struggle. Explaining the party's task in the labour field, Charu said: "It is not our task either to organise trade unions, or to bring them under our control, or to bother ourselves about the trade union elections. Our task is to build secret party organization among the workers." Regarding the form of struggle, Charu Mazumdar said: "While we should encourage the workers in any struggle they wage we must, nonetheless, constantly explain to them that, today, the weapons like *hartals* and strikes have become largely blunted in dealing with the attacks of the organized capitalist class (such as lock-out, lay-off, closure etc.). Today, the struggles can no longer develop peacefully or without bloodshed. To develop, the struggles must take the forms of *gherao*, clash with the police and the capitalists, barricade fights, annihilating the class enemies and their agents etc. according to the given conditions."[3]

Thus the CPI(ML)'s desperate drive to step up the armed struggle in India and its exhortation to the students and youth and workers to plunge into the revolutionary struggle contributed to sharpening the edge of Naxalite violence.

71

'Cultural Revolution'

The young generation responded to Charu's clarion call by carrying out raids on educational institutions, boycotting examinations, disfiguring the statues of national leaders and hoisting red flags. Charu Mazumdar justified the attacks on schools and colleges on the ground that the present educational system was a "colossal fraud". According to him, those who received the so-called education were mostly fed on lies during the most impressionable years of their lives. Far from being imparted any revolutionary concepts, their minds were stuffed with reactionary ideas. What the students and youth were doing was therefore "just and proper". The "festival of idol smashing" was justified by him in the following words:

> "The people of India fought to overthrow British rule; many heroes laid down their lives in the course of struggle. But they have not been depicted as models, their images have not been installed: on the contrary it is those who have served and defended the interests of imperialism are held up before the students and the people as models and whose images have been built. That is why those who accuse the students and youths of waging war against the national tradition are in reality singing hymns in praise of the tradition created by imperialism's lackeys. A genuinely patriotic, revolutionary India cannot be built unless the images of these lackeys are swept away. This is why these deeds of the students and youths are, without doubt, revolutionary deeds and are, without doubt, preparing the path of India's progress."[4]

The images of people who allegedly served the interests of imperialists, comprador bourgeoisie and the feudal class represented, according to Charu, "rival, antagonistic class interests and ideologies". It was therefore necessary to destroy those images. As to the charge that the students were committing excesses in their acts of vandalism, Charu quoted from Mao's Hunan report to say that "to right a wrong, it is necessary to exceed the proper limits".

The images and portraits disfigured or destroyed included those of recognised leaders like Mahatma Gandhi, Rabindra Nath Tagore, Iswar Chandra Vidyasagar, Ashutosh Mukherji, Jawahar Lal Nehru,

Lal Bahadur Shastri and several others. The party's assessment was that they all sided with the "enemies of the people" and did not support the peasants' revolt or uphold the cause of people struggling to over- throw the mountains of imperialism and feudalism. About Mahatma Gandhi, it was said that his entire life was "one long inglorious career of devoted service to imperialism, feudalism and the comprador bour- geoisie". He was denigrated as a "traitor" who served the British im- perialists by recruiting Indian soldiers to defend the British Empire during World War, disarmed the Indian people with his "spurious" theory of non-violence and led a movement for "sham independence".

It is an interesting comparison that around this very time Judith Miller of the Vincennes philosophy faculty was propagating similar ideas in France. "The University", he declared, "is part of the state machinery, a piece of capitalist society. Total destruction is needed. There is a crisis inside bourgeois society and we must accelerate this crisis".[5] This so-called Cultural Revolution was, however, criticised by an influential section within the party. Sushital Roy Choudhury questioned the wisdom of assault on the images of persons like Ram- mohun Roy and Rabindranath Tagore and wondered if it was a neces- sary prelude to the armed struggle. He also disagreed with Mazumdar's comparison of these activities with the student movement in China.

Charu Mazumdar stressed that the movement of students and youth was complementary to the revolutionary peasant struggle. It was not to be viewed in isolation but as part of the democratic revolution. In actual practice, however, the emphasis on urban actions by the students and youth led to a steady neglect of the rural areas. The cadres working in the countryside grew either lethargic or gravitated to the towns where the movement was raging in full fury.

Attacks on Police

There was gradual enlargement in the scope of the movement. There were raids on government offices accompanied by extensive damage to property and brutal attacks on policemen.

The attacks on policemen, it was argued, would serve a dual purpose. On the one hand, it would break the morale of the force and in due course lead to collapse of the bourgeois state appratus; and, on the

73

other, it would provide an excellent opportunity to seize their firearms and thereby build the armoury of the so-called People's Liberation Army. The ideological justification for the attacks was provided by Charu Mazumdar in an article 'Avenge the Heroic Martyrs' which appeared in the *Liberation* of September-December 1970. It was stated that the police in the country, trained by foreigners, had always been used as "an instrument for murdering and suppressing the people." He went even to the extent of saying that "these (policemen) are not Indians: these are not of India" and called upon the party workers to "rouse the intensest hatred for all these cowards, imperialism's running dogs and assassins." Besides, with the peasants' struggles acquring the character of a liberation war, it was necessary to attack the armed forces of the enemy. "To wage attacks now against only class enemies amounts to a certain form of economism. If we fail to wage attacks against the armed forces of the enemy simultaneously with our attacks on these class enemies we shall land ourselves in the mire of a certain kind of economism." And so the Communist revolutionaries were asked "not only to wipe out the police force but to seize their rifles and to arm the squads of the peasant guerillas with those rifles."

It is estimated that during the period 1970-71, a total of 75 policemen were annihilated by the Naxalites, most of them in West Bengal

Lumpen Infiltration

In the pervasive atmosphere of violence, the lumpen elements infiltrated the Naxalite ranks. The party workers welcomed them because of their expertise in annihilations and failed to realise the long-term effects of their induction on the character and ethos of the movement. Ranjit Gupta, then Commissioner of Police, Calcutta says that the Naxalite killings increased several-fold and it was obvious from the style and technique of murders that "the anti-socials had come into business."[6] The total number of people killed during the period March 1970 to June 15, 1971 in Calcutta City, according to the Commissioner, were:

CPI(M) supporters	44
Congress(R)	4
Forward Bloc	2

CPI	1
Government employees	2
Home Guards	8
Persons suspected to be informers	12
Basti owners	1
Businessmen	14
Moneylenders	2
Unclassified	21
Policemen	28
Total	139

The businessmen, moneylenders and *basti* landlords constituted only 12 per cent of the total killings. The urban class enemy, it would seem, was by and large left out. The political rivals represented a much higher 37 per cent. In rural areas, on the other hand, the class enemies (businessmen and *jotedars*) killed constituted 40 per cent of the total people killed.

The induction of anti-social elements had a deleterious effect on the organisational discipline and ideological orientation of the party. It is surprising that the Naxalite leaders, in this context, ignored the warnings of their own godfathers. Marx had described them as "thieves and criminals of all kinds living on the crumbs of society". Engels had said that "this scum of the depraved elements of all classes, which establishes headquarters in the big cities, is the worst of all possible allies. The rabble is absolutely venal and absolutely brazen... Every leader of the workers who uses these scoundrels as guards or relies on them for support proves himself by this action alone a traitor to the movement". Mao had, however, at one place conceded that "they can become a revolutionary force when properly guided". But here guidance there was none. The anti-social scum used the Naxalite umbrella to settle their old scores. The movement, in the process, got disoriented.

People's Liberation Army

Charu Mazumdar was, however, undaunted and he relentlessly and ruthlessly drove the party cadres along. Towards the end of 1970, he mentioned, for the first time, the proposal to form a People's Liberation Army.

"I do not indulge in day-dreaming when I say that by 1970-71, the People's Liberation Army will march across a vast area of West Bengal...The Chinese People's Liberation Army under the leadership of Chairman plunged into the revolutionary struggle with only 320 rifles. It may be we shall at first build our Liberation Army with 60 rifles and 200 pipe-guns."[7]

An arms-snatching incident from a police post near village Magurjan in Purnea district of Bihar on the Bihar-West Bengal border on October 27, 1970 greatly boosted the party morale. It so happened that an armed police picket posted to guard a bridge on the broad gauge railway line was attacked by a group of about 25 Naxalites. The head constable and a constable were seriously injured and six rifles with 60 rounds of ammunition were snatched away. It was a planned action by the West Bengal Naxalites who raided the place in collaboration with the local Naxalites. A few months later, on March 9, 1971, there was a more serious incident of similar nature in village Rupuskundi in the Singhbhum district of Bihar. A Bihar Military Police camp having a strength of one lance naik and 9 constables was overwhelmed by more than 50 Naxalites. They killed two constables, injured 3 others and decamped with nine rifles and 105 cartridges. These incidents emboldened the CPI(ML) to announce, in early 1971, the formation of the People's Liberation Army:

"In this excellent revolutionary situation the Indian People's Liberation Army has been founded. It is out of the many guerilla squads of landless and poor peasants who have been waging revolutionary armed struggle in various parts of West Bengal under the leadership of Charu Mazumdar and the Communist Party of India (Marxist-Leninist) that the People's Liberation Army has emerged... The capture of rifles and bullets from an armed police camp at Magurjan in the Naxalbari area by peasant guerillas and the formation of the People's Liberation Army, which welds together all the scattered squads of poor and landless peasants, mark a decisive turning point in the history of the Indian revolution. Led by the Party, the PLA, now a small force, will grow from strength to strength as it will fight and annihilate the enemy and

76

his armed forces, conduct propaganda among the masses, organise them, arm them and help them to establish revolutionary political power. The sole purpose of this army will be to stand firmly with the Indian people and to serve them whole heartedly."[8]

The CPI(ML) claimed that with the formation of the People's Liberation Army, "the peasants' revolutionary armed struggle has reached a new stage—a qualitatively higher stage. This is the stage when the destruction of the armed forces of the reactionary state and the establishment of people's revolutionary political power is on the agenda".

The naivete in Charu Mazumdar's assessment of the Indian situation and his attempt to make the seventies the decade of liberation was indeed amazing or even pathetic. The people of India were not yet ready for revolution and the ruling class was well entrenched with formidable resources and enormous powers at their command. History has its own inexorable pace and it was puerile on the part of Charu Mazumdar to have thought that he could accelerate it and achieve the liberation of India by 1975. Even according to Mao, "Marxists are not fortune-tellers. They should, and indeed can, only indicate the general direction of future developments and changes; they should not and cannot fix the day and the hour in a mechanistic way." The People's Liberation Army, whose formation was trumpeted, existed only on the pages of *Liberation*. The few arms snatched by Naxalite guerillas and the countrymade weapons they were asked to rely upon were no match to the superior fire-power of the police and the para-military forces.

Nevertheless, the bold announcements and the loud declarations of the CPI(ML) were accompanied by a spurt in violent activities. According to a rough estimate, there were a total of about 4,000 incidents in the country from the middle of 1970 to the middle of 1971. The bulk of these were from West Bengal (3,500) followed by Bihar (220) and Andhra Pradesh (70).

The Government of India was forced to take stock of the situation. It got in touch with the states most affected and formulated plans to contain the Naxalite violence.

5

THE FLICKER

5.1 CRACKS IN THE PARTY

For a revolutionary, failure is a springboard.
As a source of theory it is richer than victory:
it accumulates experience and knowledge.
                                                    —Regis Debray

The Government of India decided to undertake joint operations by the army and the police in the bordering districts of West Bengal, Bihar and Orissa which were particularly affected by Naxalite depredations. The operations were undertaken from July 1 to August 15, 1971 and were code-named 'Operation Steeplechase'.[1]

The broad strategy of the Security Forces was to surround as large an area as possible and seal the routes of entry and exit. The army formed the outer cordon and the C.R.P.F. the inner ring. The local police, which was generally accompanied by a magistrate, carried out thorough search of the area. Suspected Naxalites were arrested, illicit weapons, ammunition and explosives seized. Wherever possible, simultaneous action was taken in the neighbouring area also so that the Naxalites sneaking out were caught while attempting to escape. Such information as was gleaned in the course of operations was followed up by subsequent action. These operations covered Midnapur, Purulia, Burdwan and Birbhum districts of West Bengal; Singhbhum, Dhanbad and Santhal Parganas of Bihar, and Mayurbhanj of Orissa. In West Bengal, the operations extended over the entire period of 45 days, but in Bihar and Orissa the duration was much shorter.

The 'Operation Steeplechase' achieved the desired results, though not to the extent anticipated by the administration. The organisational apparatus of the Naxalites in the aforesaid districts was thrown out of gear and the party activists fled from their known hide-outs to other places in search of safety. Violence registered a drop. Incidents of arms-snatching fell down. Above all, it restored the confidence of the people in the strength of the administration. It was however felt that the effectiveness of the operation was squandered by its premature publicity which gave the Naxalite activists time to escape. Besides, only a section could be arrested; the bulk of them were merely flushed out. In Birbhum, for example, of the 400 known Naxalite activists, only about 150 were caught. Nevertheless the fact remains that the operation stemmed the advancing tide of Naxalism and disrupted the Communist extremists' organisational network in the worst affected areas of the three states.

Internal differences within the party were meanwhile having a disintegrating effect. The CPI (ML) was doubtless the most important component of the extremist movement in the country, but it did not represent all the shades of extremism. Charu Mazumdar compounded the problem by his inability to carry the team along. He had the intellectual brilliance but not the organisational skill to keep the heterogeneous elements together—and the CPI(ML) soon became a house divided. Charu's policy of reckless terrorism in the urban areas and frenzied attempts to achieve the liberation of India by 1975, resulting in the loss of precious cadres, coupled with the moves to arrogate all powers in himself in disregard of the Politburo and the Central Committee, led to heated debates within the party. Discordant voices soon began to be heard. The differences surfaced for the first time at the Party Congress, where Charu Mazumdar made a pointed attack on the 'centrists'. He assailed them for disagreeing with the party line on annihilation of class enemies and the use of firearms.

Introducing the political and organisational report at the Party Congress, Charu Mazumdar underscored that the "battle of annihilation is both a higher form of class struggle and the starting point of guerilla war." He chided those who, while agreeing that annihilation is the starting point of guerilla war, did not concur with the view that it was a higher form of class struggle and also others who carried on the struggle for the seizure of landlords' land and property without waging the battle of annihilation. On the use of firearms, Charu Mazumdar felt that dependence on them would stifle the initiative of the peasants and therefore he showed his preference for conventional weapons like knives, choppers, swords and spears. Charu Mazumdar felt that if they started the battle of annihilation with these traditional weapons, the common landless and poor peasants would be encouraged to join the guerilla fighters and "their revolutionary enthusiasm will know no bounds."

The dissidents, however, continued to snipe at Charu Mazumdar[2]. They denounced his policies as a perversion and vulgarisation of Marxism-Leninism. The attack was spearheaded by Sushital Roy Choudhury of West Bengal, Satyanaryan Singh of Bihar and Shiv Kumar Mishra of U P.

The Chinese Communist Party is also believed to have sent a note to CPI(ML) in November 1970, conveying their disagreement with certain aspects of CPI(ML)'s policies. Souren Bose, Central Committee Member, had sneaked to Peking in 1970, travelling through Albania, Karachi and Dhaka. The message was actually brought by him. Charu Mazumdar however suppressed the communication because it would have undermined his position vis-a-vis the dissidents. A note later circulated jointly by Kanu Sanyal, Chowdhary Tejeswara Rao, Souren Bose, D. Nagabhushanam Patnaik, Kolla Venkaiah and D. Bhuvan Mohan Patnaik disclosed that the Chinese Communist Party had criticised China's Chairman being called Chairman of the CPI(ML) as "it will wound the national sentiment of the working class of this country"; that Charu's concept of United Front was wrong; that the annihilation theory needed re-thinking; that Lin-Biao's People's War Theory had been applied to Indian conditions in a mechanical way and that mass struggle and mass organisation were necessary for sustaining the armed struggle. The general orientation of CPI(ML) was correct but its policy was wrong. The signatories called upon all the members of the party to repudiate "the Left adventurist, deviationist line advocated by Comrade Charu Mazumdar."[3] The contents of Chinese criticism were however known only after Charu's death. Meanwhile the intra-party debate continued.

Charu Mazumdar was accused of setting himself up as an" oracle of Indian revolution" and elevating himself above the party. There was a subtle move at the Party Congress to establish the revolutionary authority of Charu Mazumdar. A campaign for this was actually started in early 1970 itself. The Liberation of February 1970 contained a full length article entitled *To Win Victory in the Revolution we Must Establish the Revolutionary Authority*. Starting from the premise that "there can be no revolution without a Revolutionary Authority," it made out a strong case for placing Mazumdar on a pedestal comparable to that of Mao in China. The argument ran on the following lines:

"From the initiation of the Naxalbari struggle to the building of the Party, strengthening of the Party by fighting against the hidden enemies in it and the leadership given by the Party over the armed struggle all over India—each of these events bears the indelible imprint of the able, correct and successful leadership given by our respected and beloved leader Comrade Charu Mazumdar, leadership which has grown still richer and firmer through the summing up of the experience of the Indian revolution.

Our task today is to establish firmly the authority of the leadership of Comrade Charu Mazumdar at all levels of the Party and revolution."

The move was, however, fiercely resisted at the Party Congress by the delegates from U.P, Bihar, Tamil Nadu and Assam. The Charu group was obliged to beat a retreat and withdraw the resolution on the subject. The dissidents were neverthless dissatisfied as they felt that the Politburo and the Central Committee had been relegated to the background and all powers centralised in Charu Mazumdar. Charu's argument that the insurgent conditions in the country, with the police hunting for the Naxalites all over, did not permit the convening of a meeting and that a get-together of the leaders would be hazardous for their security did not carry conviction with the dissidents. They felt that these were specious pleas of Charu to side-track the party's representative bodies and conduct its affairs in a manner and style of his own choosing. Denouncing Charu Mazumdar's authoritarianism, the Satyanarayan Singh group drew attention to the fundamentals of party discipline as enunciated by Mao Tse-tung, viz. that the individual is subordinate to the organisation; the minority is subordinate to the majority; the lower committees are subordinate to the higher committees; and all party members are subordinate to the Central Committee.

Charu was also attacked for ignoring the need of base areas and maintaining that "it is the enemy who is in need of finding out the base areas for his self-preservation and not revolutionaries." The dissidents however argued on the authority of Mao that base areas were essential for the guerilla forces to perform their strategic tasks and achieve their objective of preserving and expanding themselves and destroying and driving out the enemy. The S.N. Singh group stated that it would give top priority to the task of building up rural base areas, particularly in the mountainous and forest regions and in the river valley areas. It however clarified that they would not vacate the plains and would continue armed struggle there also. Charu Mazumdar's advice to start as many points of armed struggle as possible—"Don't try to concentrate. Expand anywhere and everywhere"— was held alien to Mao's Thought and the path of people's war.

Charu Mazumdar was further criticised for defying Mao's theory that a people's democratic revolution should precede a socialist revolution and trying to accomplish both the revolutions in one stroke. The S.N. Singh group also contested Charu Mazumdar's view that a revolutionary united front was possible only after establishing liberated zones and branded this as "close doorism" of the worst kind. The dissidents felt that if this "Trotskyite line" was put into practice, the party would get miserably isolated. They expounded their concept of a United Front in the following words:

"Contrary to the thesis advocated by the Charu clique, the Central Committee maintains that the leader of the new democratic revolution is the working class. The Central Committee maintains that the working class fully relies on the landless and the poor peasants, firmly unites with the middle peasants, wins over a section of the rich peasants while neutralising the rest. The understanding of the Central Committee is that only a tiny section of the rich peasants may join the enemy camp. The Central Committee considers the urban petty bourgeoisie as a reliable ally of the working class and the national bourgeois as an ally to some extent and in certain periods."[4]

Charu's line of going in for frontal clashes, giving up all ideas of self-defence, concentrating on self-sacrifice only and not worrying about the losses was also assailed. It was alleged that he was deliberately confusing the tactical thinking with the strategical thinking. The dissidents were of the view that tactically the revolutionaries must view the enemy seriously and assess his strength carefully, though strategically they might despise him. "Not to regard the enemy as paper tiger, strategically, is Right opportunism, and not to regard the enemy as a real tiger, tactically, is Left opportunism." It followed, as a corollary, that the dissidents did not subscribe to Charu Mazumdar's theory of "quick victory" and his plan to achieve the liberation of India by 1975. This, they said, amounted to rejecting the strategy and tactics of people's war. They emphasised that notwithstanding the rapid strides made by the Naxalite movement, armed struggle in the country was still in its infancy, the number of guerilla squads was very small and the building up of the Red Army had yet to be undertaken. The S. N. Singh group categorically declared that the Chinese path of protracted people's war was valid for India and there could be no short-cut to the Indian revolution.

The urban actions unleashed in Calcutta and other towns of West Bengal met with particularly strong disapproval of Charu's critics. They criticised his programme of destroying schools, colleges, libraries and laboratories; breaking up the idols of gods and goddesses; attacking clubs and recreation halls; annihilating small or middle traders, businessmen, merchants and capitalists; and annihilating the cadres of revisionist parties. The dissidents felt that this programme had disrupted the unity of the toiling masses and isolated CPI (ML) from the broad masses of the people. They also accused Charu Mazumdar of neglecting party work in the rural areas by concentrating in Calcutta and other cities. It was stressed by them that party work in the cities should be complementary to the task of building up rural base areas and that it should come at par with work in the rural areas only in the final phase of revolution when decisive battles would be waged for the capture of cities. For the present, in the words of S.N. Singh group, "as the cities are the strongholds of the enemy, we must transform the rural areas into our strongholds militarily, politically, economically and culturally."

Another point of disagreement was Charu's boycott of the economic struggles on the ground that "guerilla struggle is the only form of class struggle." The dissidents felt that they should not be shy of joining and supporting demonstrations, gheraos, slow-downs, strikes, etc. on economic issues and, on the contrary, fight as its vanguard. They expressed the view that while the line of confining people's struggle to economic issues was Right opportunism, the line of boycotting economic struggle in the name of political struggle amounted to Left opportunism. "The correct line is to make the economic and political struggles complementary to the revolutionary armed struggle." Mao's formulation that "stressing armed struggle does not mean abandoning other forms of struggle; on the contrary, armed struggle cannot succeed unless coordinated with other forms of struggle" was quoted by them in support of their contention.

The liberation struggle in East Pakistan leading to the emergence of Bangla Desh exacerbated the divisions in the CPI (ML) and led to parting of the ways. China's support to the Pak military regime caused considerable confusion among the extremist ranks. The Chinese, to start with, maintained an eloquent silence on the developments in East Pakistan. China's dilemma was understandable. It had, over a period of years, cultivated close relations with Pakistan as a counter-weight to India. On the other hand, Peking had always sworn by liberation movements of oppressed peoples. *Hsinhua*, the official press agency, published the first news on the crisis in Pakistan on April 4, 1971, but it was non-committal. The agency merely reported President Yahya Khan's announcement about sending troops to East Pakistan and Pakistan's allegations of Indian interference in its affairs. On April 6, the Chinese Embassy in New Delhi lodged a protest with the Government of India over a demonstration held in front of its premises earlier on March 29, charging India of interfering in Pakistan's internal affairs and conniving at provocations by several hundred Indians in front of the Chinese Embassy. The protest was significant on two counts: it was lodged eight days after the demonstration, and it accused the demonstrators of slandering China for aiding the Pakistan Government in its war on the freedom loving people of East Bengal. By implication, it amounted to saying that China was not helping Pakistan and, besides, East Bengalis were "freedom loving" people and not secessionists. The first clear indication of Peking's endorsement of West Pakistan's stand was contained in a commentator's article published in the *People's Daily* of April 11. Written under the caption *What are the Indian Expansionists planning to do?*, the article accused the Government of India of interfering in the internal affairs of Pakistan and expressed support for the government and people of Pakistan in their "just struggle for safeguarding national independence and state sovereignty and against foreign aggression and interference."

The support to Islamabad was further reinforced by a message sent by Chou En-lai to Yahya Khan on April 12. The Chinese Premier observed that "the unification of Pakistan and the unity of the people of East and West Pakistan are the basic guarantees for Pakistan to attain prosperity and strength." He clarified the Chinese Government's stand that what was happening in Pakistan was "purely the internal affair of Pakistan which can only be settled by Pakistani people themselves and which brooks no foreign interference whatsoever." Chou En-lai went on to assure the Pak authorities that "should the Indian expansionists dare to launch aggression against Pakistan, the Chinese Government and people will always firmly support the Pakistan Government and people in their just struggle to safeguard state sovereignty and national independence."[5]

Ideological consistency apart, China's policy was certainly in keeping with its national interests. It has been rightly pointed out that ever since 1949 China had been seeking to gain recognition of its sovereignty over those minority areas which could harbour and nourish separatist national movements[6]. In Tibet, it forestalled this danger by both diplomatic and military measures, though in Sinkiang it was not able to ward off completely the threat of a Soviet-sponsored separatist movement. Besides, China had always upheld the goal of unification for the two Germanys, the two Vietnams and the two Koreas. The Chinese policy could, however, be faulted for placing national interests above ideological considerations. The Chinese had supported the FLN government in Algeria, the Provisional Government of the NLF in South Vietnam and the emigre government of Prince Sihanouk of Cambodia.

The CPI (ML) spelt out its views on the struggle in Bangla Desh in the *Deshabroti* of April 28, 1971. The salient points of the party's stand were as follows:

i)   The Government of India is ready to attack Pakistan. It is already directing the Mukti Yudha and running the so-called Bangla Desh Government from West Bengal.

ii) India is actually being instigated by the U.S.A., USSR and other imperialist powers in furtherance of their anti-China designs. Pakistan has refused to join this conspiracy even though it is a member of several imperialist pacts.

iii) The imperialists engineered the "armed mutiny" in East Bengal.

iv) Mujibur Rehman is an imperialist agent and has therefore not protested against Pakistani capitalism or demanded distribution of land from *jotedars* to the peasants.

v) The Government of India's concern for the refugees is hypocritical. It is like "robbing Peter to pay Paul" in the sense that the money collected from the exploitation of the Indian people would be utilised to extend benefits to the refugees.

vi) The East Pakistan Communist Party (ML) has started peasants' armed struggle which has spread over eight districts. This struggle is limited in dimensions but is bound to spread throughout the country.

The above analysis concluded with an exhortation that the revolutionaries of India, particularly those of West Bengal, should crush this conspiracy and demand stoppage of armed intervention and freedom to the people of East Pakistan to decide their own fate.

The Naxalite ranks and file however did not accept these formulations. They wondered how Peking could support the military junta of Pakistan, riding roughshod over the wishes of the toiling masses of Bangla Desh. Sheikh Mujibur Rehman was a popular leader and the Awami League was spearheading what was essentially a liberation movement. The fact that the movement was not led by Maoists did not affect its basic character. The Chinese stand to them smacked of unabashed political opportunism. It appeared to be a classic case of China giving precedence to its regional interests over ideological considerations. The Naxalite cadres were, as a consequence, greatly disillusioned. A survey carried out by the *Hindustan Times* correspondents[7] in some states clearly brought out that the CPI (ML) leaders and workers were deserting the party. In the southern states of Andhra Pradesh, Mysore, Tamil Nadu and Kerala, large number of them were reported to be joining other revolutionary groups. A number of party workers in Srikakulam joined the Revolutionary Communist Group of Nagi

Reddy. In West Bengal also, the Naxalites showed signs of uneasiness and disenchantment[8]. The process of disillusionment was accelerated by other leftist parties interested in winning over the Naxalite ranks. The CPI organ *New Age* made a blistering attack on China in its editorial of April 18, 1971:

"It is an indelible shame that the Chinese leaders who still swear by Communism should have stooped to such depths of ideological and moral degradation. For all their affection for Yahya Khan even the imperialists are hesitating to openly support him. This ideological and political degeneration of the present Chinese leadership is however not a sudden lapse. It is a product of big power chauvinism and Machiavellism which have been substituted for Marxism-Leninism. Today these leaders have so forgotten the revolutionary tradition and heritage of the Chinese people that they do not have even a twinge of conscience when the issue involved in Bangla Desh is the very survival of 75 million people ruthlessly plundered and oppressed for nearly quarter of a century by a clique of militarists, bureaucrats, monopolists and big landlords. Yet Peking leaders have the gumption to claim that they are the greatest champions of national liberation.

Would Peking's stand on the Bangla Desh issue open the eyes of the Naxalites, who are damaging themselves and more so India's Communist movement by their blind adherence to the Maoist commandments? If for nothing else, at least for the sake of 75 million people of Bangla Desh, so heroically struggling for their freedom and even for their human rights, the Naxalites should liberate themselves from Peking's spell before thinking of liberating others. The support of Bangla Desh struggle and the loyalty to the Peking leadership cannot obviously go together."

The message went home and a sizeable chunk of the Naxalite cadres sought refuge under other political umbrellas.

In a last-ditch effort to maintain unity and curb indiscipline in the ranks, Charu Mazumdar started taking stringent action. He removed Sushital Roy Choudhury from the editorship of *Liberation*, the CPI (ML) mouth-piece, and expelled Satyanarayan Singh, Shiv Kumar Mishra, Mahendra Singh, Gurubux Singh, Raj Kishore Singh and Ashim Chatterjee from the Central Committee. Charu even dissolved the UP and Bihar State Committees and the Bengal-Bihar-Orissa Border Area Regional Committee and formed parallel committees for these regions. These disciplinary measures were more than what the dissidents could absorb. They therefore formed a Central Committee of their own, appointing Satyanarayan Singh as General Secretary at a meeting of the anti-Charu elements held on November 7, 1971. This particular meeting also took the extreme step of expelling Charu Mazumdar and Suniti Ghosh from the Party. Thus, within a year and a half of the Party Congress, the CPI (ML) was split, with one faction owing allegiance to Charu Mazumdar and the other swearing loyalty to Satyanarayan Singh.

All this while, government pressure on the Naxalites was steadily building up. The Prime Minister, Mrs Indira Gandhi, declared in the Rajya Sabha on August 11, 1970 that the government was committed to putting down the activities of Naxalites and other extremist elements "with all the strength at its command." These elements would be "fought to the finish", she said. The 'Operation Steeplechase' (July-August 1971) had already broken the backbone of Naxalites in the worst affected bordering areas of West Bengal, Bihar and Orissa. By the first quarter of 1972, almost all the top Naxalite leaders had been apprehended by the police. Kanu Sanyal, Jangal Santhal, Nagabhushanam Patnaik, Kunnikkal Narayanan, Ashim Chatterjee and a host of others had fallen into the police net. There were about 1,400 Naxalites in jail in Andhra Pradesh, about 2,000 in Bihar, about 4,000 in Bengal and 1,000 in Kerala, UP and elsewhere[9].

Charu Mazumdar was also arrested by the Calcutta Police detectives from the Entally area of East Calcutta in the early hours of July 16, 1972. He was a shattered man by that time; his lieutenants had already deserted him. I had occasion to meet him before he breathed his last. It was amazing that such a lean and frail man had so much of fire within him. He was crest-fallen and also perhaps disillusioned. He could see that it was the end of the road for him. He knew that the revolution he wanted to bring about had failed. But there was no trace of remorse or regret at the course of action he had charted for himself and the revolutionary cadres who gravitated towards him.

He appeared to me, in Arnold's words, "a beautiful but ineffectual angel beating his luminous wings in the void in vain." A few days later, on July 28, Charu Mazumdar breathed his last.

It would be an exaggeration to describe Charu as India's Mao, but the fact remains that he is tallest among those Indians of the post-Independence era who attempted to bring about an armed revolution in the country to overthrow a system which they sincerely felt had failed. However, he was not pragmatic and therefore tried to jump several stages and achieve the liberation of India within a very short time-frame without mobilising the masses or building up a well trained and well equipped liberation army. He under-estimated the strength of the state apparatus which came down heavily on the Naxalite cadres, resulting in the cream of India's youth being sacrificed in several areas. The slogan 'China's Chairman is our Chairman, China's path is our path' was the height of short-sightedness. Any movement should have its roots in the soil; it must draw inspiration from the history and culture of the land itself.

Biplab Dasgupta has aptly summed up the weaknesses of the Naxalite movement and the factors which led to its decline in the following words:

"The principal weakness of the Naxalites was their belief that the people of India would rise up in revolt as soon as they had lit the spark of armed struggle. In the tactic of indvidual annihilation they thought they had found an alternative to mass organisation and mass ideological propaganda. Initially, the annihilation policy was a success. As soon as two or three landlords were killed, the others ran away to the safety of the towns or became ardent supporters of the Naxalites overnight. These killings created a power vacuum in the villages and the Naxalites stepped in to fill the void. The Naxalites described these areas as 'liberated' because they could move around freely within their boundaries. But soon the number of murders of class enemies became the criterion by which the Naxalites began judging the revolutionary tempo of a locality. Whenever an annihilation took place in a new area, the event was equated with the spread of revolution to that area.

The guerillas did not take the masses into confidence in the 'liberated' areas. The assassinations were done by a handful of activists, the criminal elements in the villages were drawn towards the movement and the economic demands of the villagers were ignored. All these facors alienated the Naxalites further from the masses. The Naxalites also understimated 'white terror' and over-estimated their own strength. They had very few, almost no training in guerilla warfare and ideology and, worst of all, the people were not on their side in their conflict with the police. The police force met with feeble resistance when it entered these 'liberated' areas and was brutal in its suppression of the movement."[10]

Charu's death, in any case, marked the end of a phase in the Naxalite movement which had convulsed large parts of the country for nearly five years.

5.2   POST-MAZUMDAR PERIOD

Wandering between two worlds, one dead,
The other powerless to be born.

—Matthew Arnold

The period following the death of Charu Mazumdar witnessed subdivisions and fragmentations in the Naxalite movement. Broadly speaking, there were two sets of groups—one which continued to owe allegiance to Charu Mazumdar and his ideology and the other which was opposed to it. The pro-Mazumdar Naxalites were further subdivided into pro-Lin Biao and anti-Lin Biao factions. It is necessary to clarify the basis of this ideological divide. Lin Biao, who was at one stage considered the successor to Mao and his "closest comrade in arms," in a lengthy thesis entitled *Long Live The Victory Of The People's War* (September 1965) upheld the Maoist model of revolution for the third world. He emphasised that "Mao Tse-tung's theory of the establishment of rural revolutionary base areas and the encirclement of the cities from the countryside is of outstanding and universal practical significance for the present revolutionary struggles of the oppressed nations and peoples in Asia, Africa and Latin America." Lin's strategy was to merge the people's wars in the Third World into a "torrential world-wide tide." His thesis made a powerful impact on the Naxalites in India and was taken by them as the green signal for a people's war in India. Subsequently, however, at the Tenth Congress of the Communist Party of China (August 1973) Lin Biao was denigrated and, what was most embarrassing, Chou En-lai's political report made no mention of the armed struggle in India. (Earlier, the Ninth Congress had expressed its "firm support" for the revolutionary struggles in several countries including India). It was the Chinese way of conveying their disapproval of Mazumdar's tactical line. In any case, Lin Biao's disgrace was a great blow to the CPI (ML) because the Naxalite approach to guerilla warfare was based on Lin's assertion that it was "the only way to mobilise and apply the entire strength of the people against the enemy". The followers of Charu Mazumdar who continued to stick to the Lin Biao thesis and believed that Chinese criticism of Mazumdar was because of internal dissensions in the CPC came to be known as the Pro-Lin Biao Group. The other faction which also owed allegiance to Charu Mazumdar but accepted the Chinese criticism came to be known as the Anti-Lin Biao Group.

The Pro-Lin Biao Group was led by Mahadeb Mukherjee. It held the Second Congress of the party in December 1973 whereat the party programme of 1970 was reaffirmed as "the only correct programme for the entire period of India's People's Democratic Revolution and which most aptly and boldly upholds the correct line of Comrade Lin Biao." This group embarked on a programme of annihilations, gun snatchings, jail breaks, and attacks on policemen. There were altogether 54 violent incidents in West Bengal in 1973 in which 10 policemen were killed and 39 firearms snatched from different places. The cadres appeared to be more desperate in their attacks, but their activities were neither planned nor orchestrated with the result that the state police got the better of them. It is also a fact that people in general, alienated by senseless terrorism, were now cooperating with the police. As a result, the extremists had great difficulty in finding shelter and were always running from pillar to post. The rifles snatched from the Mayapur police camp on July 25, 1974 were recovered within a short time after an encounter in which four extremists were killed. The police surprised the extremists at several other places like Bandel, Pandua and Santoshpur, and arms and ammunition were recovered.

The Anti-Lin Biao Group, which held its own Second Congress in March 1973, issued a statement congratulating the Chinese Communist Party on successful conclusion of the Tenth Congress which had "consolidated the victory of the proletariat over the anti-party clique led by Lin Biao, the bourgeois-careerist, double-dealer, spy and traitor." The party acknowledged Mazumdar's death as a great loss and admitted that there was, "setback because the party committed certain errors."

The Anti-Lin Biao Group figured prominently in the Bhojpur district of Bihar. Here the lower castes lived in conditions of extreme poverty and were subjected to social exploitation also. As described by Kalyan Mukherjee and Rajendra Singh Yadav:

"...the oppression of the lower castes at the hands of the upper castes did not flow from numerical superiority but rather from niches in the economic hierarchy apropos land ownership and the monopoly over labour. Further the culture of violence ensured that the Chamar or the Musahar never raises his head in protest.

Though *begar* was a thing of the past, the *banihar* worked often for nothing. Wearing a clean *dhoti*, remaining seated in the presence of the master even on a cot outside his own hut, walking erect were taboo. When the evenings fell or in lonely stretches of field, the rape of his womenfolk by landlord's *latheiths* and scions completed a picture of unbridled Rajput-Bhumihar overlordship."[1]

The lower castes comprising Ahirs, Kurmis and Koeris were organised by Jagdish Mahto, a school teacher, and Rameshwar Ahir, an ex-convict, and the first annihilation took place on February 23, 1971 when Sheopujan Singh, a notorious *latheith* of the landlord of Ekwari was killed. On March 30, another landlord Jagdish Singh was murdered while returning from the fields. Other killings followed, and it is estimated that during the period 1971 to 1977, the Naxalites killed about 90 landlords. On March 14, 1974, seven policemen were injured when about 40 Naxalites swooped on a police party in Chilhoas village in Sandesh police circle of Bhojpur district, snatching 3 rifles and 20 cartridges. The Sahar, Sandesh, Tarai and Udwantnagar blocks of the district were particularly affected. Ekwari in Sahar block came to be known as the 'Naxalbari of Bhojpur'. In 1975, according to the District Superintendent of Police, the following number of villages, thana-wise, were strongly held by Naxalites:[2]

Sahar	– 39
Sandesh	– 29
Piro	– 23
Tarai	– 15
Jagdishpur	– 06
Jawanagar	– 06
Udwantnagar	– 06
Brahmpur	– 05

Eighty per cent of the landless peasants of the district, according to the police, were "sympathisers or activists" of the Naxalite movement. The movement however collapsed after the Bihar Military Police and the Central Reserve Police conducted extensive operations—'Operation Thunder'—in the district. Rameshwar Ahir was killed in an encounter and Jagdish Mahto was killed by the villagers in an incident where they mistook him to be a dacoit.

A small group of Naxalites in Srikakulam, known as the COC (ML) and led by Suniti Kumar Ghosh and Appalasuri, also owed allegiance to Charu Mazumdar.

Among the groups opposed to Charu Mazumdar was the Andhra faction known as UCCRI (ML), popularly known as the Nagi Reddy group. This was, in fact, the first group which had challenged the ideological formulations of Charu Mazumdar. They felt that their stand had been vindicated with the CPI (ML) being almost decimated. The largest anti-Charu Mazumdar group, however, was the one led by Satyanarayan Singh. It has already been mentioned that the dissidents, breaking away from the parent body, had formed a parallel CPI (ML) with Satyanarayan Singh as the general secretary.

Satyanarayan Singh's first task was to demolish 'Charuism' and come out with a fresh set of formulations which would be in keeping with the objective conditions prevailing in the country. He had to spell out his attitude on the sensitive issue of annihilation of class enemies. This had been the cardinal principle and the battle-cry of Charu. Satyanarayan Singh tread his path very carefully. Initially he was reluctant to oppose the annihilation line. He talked of "punishing" the landlords and usurers and the corrupt officials without clarifying whether this punishment could take the form of annihilation. It was not until April 1975 that, at a meeting of the Central Committee, he formally rejected the policy of annihilation of class enemies on the ground that it had alienated the people. The other burning question at the time related to participation in elections. Here also Satyanarayan Singh brought about a gradual change in the party line. In the initial stages, he continued to repeat that there was an excellent revolutionary situation in the country and that under these conditions any participation in the democratic exercise would "divert the people from the path of armed struggle." It was however added that the path would be long and arduous, that they would have to work among the poor landless peasants to raise their political consciousness and that revolution could not be a "walk over" in the Indian conditions.

The imposition of Emergency in 1975 led to banning of almost all the Naxalite groups in the country. A large number of party workers were arrested and put inside jails. The Satyanarayan Singh group talked of overthrowing the "fascist" regime and, in December 1975, formed along with three other Naxalite groups—the Central Organising Committee of CPI (ML), the United Committee of Communist Revolutionaries of India and the Communist Unity Committee(ML)—an All India Joint Action Committee of Communist Revolutionaries. The Committee however proved to be a non-starter. There were differences among the constituents on the interpretation of the Emergency and on the kind of united front needed under the prevailing conditions. In any case, Naxalite activities during the period were on a low key.

The March 1977 election leading to the defeat of Mrs Indira Gandhi and the installation of Janata Government at the Centre opened new opportunities for the Naxalites. In a memorandum to the Prime Minister, Morarji Desai, four Naxalite groups demanded release of all political workers and withdrawal of cases and warrants of arrest against them. It was signed by Satyanarayan Singh of CPI (ML), Suniti Kumar Ghosh of Central Organising Committee, Khokan Mazumdar of the Unity Committee and Apurba Roy of the UCCRI (ML). They also pleaded for the repeal of anti-democratic measures like the MISA and the DIR, institution of judicial enquiries into all cases of killings and torture of political leaders and workers and withdrawal of para military forces from areas of people's struggle like Naxalbari, Srikakulam and Bhojpur. The Union Home Ministry, in a statement released on April 15, 1977, admitted that a total of 645 Naxalites were detained under MISA all over the country, the state-wise break-up being West Bengal 581, Kerala 38, Andhra Pradesh 14 and Tamil Nadu 12. Satyanarayan Singh met the Union Home Minister Mr Charan Singh and thereafter came out with a press statement on April 10, 1977 conveying the decision of the CPI (ML), "to offer critical support to the present Government." He also stated that they had decided "to support all the policies and measures which are patriotic and democratic and oppose all those which are not, both in the spheres of internal and external affairs."

Replying to a question whether the CPI (ML) would take part in the democratic process or not, Satyanarayan Singh replied:

"We wish to state emphatically that it is not our party which indulged in violent activities first at any stage of its activities. It is not our party which chose to go underground. It was the policy of 'kill and burn all' pursued by the Congress regime that was responsible for driving us underground. We wish to state categorically that violence is not our ideology. Our ideology is Marxism-Leninism."[3]

The press conference was held at the residence of Krishna Kant, MP, Secretary General of the All India People's Union of Civil Liberties and Democratic Rights.

The subsequent deliberations at New Delhi led to Charan Singh, Home Minister, agreeing to release all the detenus and the undertrial Naxalite prisoners who had been in jail for more than five years provided they supported Singh's press statement and resolution on similar lines passed by the Central Committee of the party; release the undertrial prisoners against whom there were no heinous charges provided they also gave a similar undertaking; and cancel all the warrants against Central Committee members of the CPI (ML) led by Satyanarayan Singh. The other extremist groups, however, reacted sharply to Satyanarayan Singh's agreement with the Union Government. Kanu Sanyal, Jangal Santhal, Ashim Chatterjee and Souren Bose issued a joint statement opposing his negotiations with the government for the release of Naxalite prisoners, branding Singh's conduct as, "counter revolutionary."

The Naxalite prisoners were freed nevertheless. The Prime Minister, Morarji Desai, announced at Ahmedabad on May 3, 1977 that the Centre had instructed all the state governments to release the Naxalites still under detention. One of the first acts of the United Front Government in West Bengal, which was voted to power in June 1977 assembly elections, was to announce the unconditional release of all the Naxalite prisoners and the withdrawal of warrants and cases pending against them. Jyoti Basu, Chief Minister, even took the initiative to secure the release of Naxalite prisoners in the states of Bihar and Andhra Pradesh.

It is interesting how the hard core Naxalites gradually veered round the view that they should participate in the elections. Satyanarayan Singh had already declared at the press conference on April 10, 1977 that the CPI (ML) would participate in the coming assembly elections. The other Naxalite leaders like Kanu Sanyal, Jangal Santhal, Ashim Chatterjee and Souren Bose also later issued a statement from the prison that boycotting elections would amount to "strengthening the hands of autocracy," and called upon the people of West Bengal to support the CPI (M) led United Front candidates in the elections. The party fielded candidates in five constituencies, three in West Bengal and one each in Bihar and Punjab. Elsewhere they supported the CPI (M) in West Bengal, the Akalis in Punjab and the Janata Party candidates at other places. Significantly, the CPI (ML) candidate in Gopiballavpur which had witnessed an armed uprising in the late sixties won the election, defeating both the CPI(M) and the Janata Party candidates. The UCCRI (ML), the COC (ML) and the Unity Committee (ML) however opposed participation in the elections on the ground that it would create ideological confusion among the cadres. Jayasree Rana, a leading figure in the civil liberties campaign in West Bengal and the wife of Santosh Rana who had been elected from Gopiballavpur, refused to support her husband and formed a new party, CPI (ML) Bolshevik, to register her protest. On the other hand, the CPI (ML) took the stand that the election campaign had enabled the party put across its message to the people and given it the opportunity to re-establish its link with the masses. It is obvious that this group of Naxalites wanted to come out of the cold and was averse to functioning in underground conditions any longer. Santosh Rana, after becoming a member of the Vidhan Sabha, said that they were regrouping for a "new movement" which they would like to keep "peaceful as far as possible."

The CPI (ML), at a meeting held at the Shahid Minar Maidan, Calcutta on April 22, 1978 to observe the foundation day of the party appealed to all the Communist revolutionaries to unite under the party's flag. Satyanarayan Singh conceded that the party had made tactical errors in the past. "No revolutionary activity could be successful without the active participation of the masses," he said. The CPI (ML) did not believe that a classless society could be established through elections. "Our participation in parliamentary democracy will help us to unmask it and attack it both from within and without," Satyanarayan Singh clarified.[4]

Naxalite unity however remained a far cry and, in 1980, there were about thirty groups functioning in different parts of the country, the important ones being CPI (ML) S.N. Singh, CPI (ML) Chandra Pulla Reddy, Pro-Lin Biao, Anti-Lin Biao, People's War Group, UCCRI(ML), OCCR Kanu Sanyal, Communist Bolshevik Party and MCC. It is significant that despite fragmentation the movement posed a challenge to the law enforcement authorities and the government was concerned over the "resurgence" of left extremist activities. The states particularly affected were Andhra Pradesh and Bihar, though incidents were reported from West Bengal, Tamil Nadu, Kerala, Tripura, Punjab, Assam, UP and Maharashtra also.[5] The graph of violence was indicating an upward trend, as the following figures would show:

	Total Incidents	Deaths
1978	163	40
1979	233	62
1980	305	84
1981	325	92
1982	399	126

The total membership of various Naxalite groups in 1980 was estimated to be around 30,000.

The history of the Naxalite movement during the ten years from 1980 to 1990 is largely a history of the Naxalite formations in Andhra Pradesh and Bihar. The People's War Group in Andhra gradually emerged as the most formidable, the most aggressive and the most lethal Naxalite group in the country, spreading its tentacles to the adjoining areas of Madhya Pradesh, Maharashtra and Orissa. Bihar was the other state which witnessed fierce Naxalite violence perpetrated by the 'New Left'. Here the distinction between class and caste quite often got blurred and there was blood-letting between antagonistic groups.

6

THE EMBERS

6.1 PEOPLE'S WAR GROUP (PWG)— ANDHRA, MADHYA PRADESH & MAHARASHTRA

The Dasehra festival has come
But it is not being celebrated by you.
Deepavali has come
But there are no deepams with you.
Sivaratri has come
and you are observing a fast.
But for you, the whole life is Sivaratri,
O Laxmamma
But for you, the whole life is Ammavasi.

—Gaddar

Andhra Pradesh

Andhra Pradesh has a radical tradition going back to the Telengana struggle of 1946-51. The Girijan awakening in Srikakulam had preceded the uprising in Naxalbari though, as Nagabhushanam Patnaik bemoaned, Charu Mazumdar "hijacked" the Srikakulam movement. The forces of the state squelched the uprising by 1970, apprehending or liquidating the leading Naxalite cadres.

The movement however continued to simmer. After Charu Mazumdar's death, some of his associates including Kondapalli Seetharamaiah, K G Sathyamurthy and Suniti Kumar Ghosh formed a Central Organising Committee in December 1972 and decided to concentrate on mobilising and organising the masses. They decided to eschew militancy till such time as the party was strong enough to embark on a course of violence. The group was nevertheless opposed to any participation in the elections. Kondapalli Seetharamaiah encouraged the party workers to commit 'money actions'—an euphemism for committing robbery or dacoity—to raise funds for the party. Seetharamaiah was arrested on April 26, 1977 in Nagpur when the police intercepted a vehicle carrying arms. The weapons were to be used for attack on a police station where some party activists were detained. He was released, but Seetharamaiah jumped bail and thereafter organised underground activities on an extensive scale. He broke away from the COC CPI (ML) and, on April 20, 1980, formed the CPI (ML) People's War Group. For the next ten years he moved from strength to strength and the People's War Group emerged as the most formidable Naxalite formation in the country.

What led to the resurgence of Naxalism in the Telengana area? The region is of course dotted with rivers, hills and forests and thus provides an ideal setting for guerilla activities. The basic reason however was the continued economic exploitation of the tribals by the landlords, traders and government officials, especially those of the Forest Department. As P.S Sundaram said:

> "The tribals owning small pieces of land are expropriated and sharecroppers impoverished. They are all kept under perpetual bondage towards repayment of a small debt supposedly taken generations ago. The forest wealth is freely smuggled out by contractors with the connivance of the forest staff. The tribals get neither a remunerative price for their forest produce nor a fair wage for their labour."[1]

The social dimensions of exploitation were far more revolting. The landlords of the region, belonging to Reddy and Velama communities, were usually addressed as *Dora* which meant a master or lord. C.Lokeswara Rao has succinctly described the high-handedness of the Doras in the following words:

> "The tyranny of *Doras* in Telengana is probably unmatched. *Dassi*, the film by Narsing Rao which bagged five national awards last year, depicts the life of a woman slave who enters the household of a *Dora* as part of the dowry of his bride. She is at the disposal of the master and his guests and she is forced to have abortions, being deprived of even the solace of a child of her own. She has to subsist

106

on what left over the cook pleases to pass on, but has to satisfy the appetite of just about any male in the master's household. Naxalite songs are replete with references to rape by landlords and to girls growing up with the knowledge of the inevitability of rape that awaits them. Some *Doras* even frown if a peasant wears his *dhoti* extending below the knee, and peasants are generally expected to bow and scrape if they happen to pass by a landlord in the village. Only a few such practices have disappeared with the passage of time, and the pace of change is slow."[2]

Besides, the aboriginal tribals of Adilabad, mainly Gonds, were greatly agitated over the influx of Lambadas from Maharashtra. There were some Lambadas in Andhra also, but the influx was caused by the keenness to avail the concessions extended in the state to Lambadas who were classified as Scheduled Tribe. In Maharashtra, the Lambadas did not enjoy the Scheduled Tribe status. Adilabad is one of the remote districts of Andhra. It juts into Maharashtra and is separated from the rest of the state by the Godavari river. An incident which happened in Indravelli in the district on May 20, 1981 caused great bitterness among the Gonds and alienated them from the establishment. The Naxalite had called a meeting of tribals at Indravelli and more than 30,000 tribals turned up. Apprehending a possible clash between the tribals and non-tribals, the administration refused permission for the meeting. The tribals were however determined to congregate. The inevitable happened—lathi charge and police firing. Thirteen Gonds were killed. The tribal anger was exploited by the PWG to consolidate its hold over the district and create safe havens for its cadres in the inaccessible villages.

Kondapalli Seetharamaiah was arrested for the second time on January 2, 1982. He was waiting at Begampet railway station in Hyderabad to board a train for Bombay when the police, tipped off by an informer, nabbed him. Seetharamaiah however managed to escape on January 4, 1984 from the prisoners' ward of the Osmania Hospital under dramatic circumstances. Henceforth he concentrated on organisational consolidation and expansion. Forest Committees were constituted for the jungle areas and Regional Committees for the plains areas. Armed squads or *dalams*, comprising six to ten members

107

each, were formed. There were about fifty *dalams* in all and these were active in the Telengana districts of Andhra Pradesh.

Seetharamaiah and K G Sathyamurthy worked in tandem till 1985. Subsequently they fell out on ideological issues. Seetharamaiah was a staunch follower of Charu Mazumdar and wanted to pursue the annihilation line. Sathyamurthy, on the other hand, was in favour of Maoism as modified by Deng Xiao-ping in China. Basically however it was a tussle for supremacy in the party. Seetharamaiah expelled K G Sathyamurthy from the party on charge of having become a victim of 'six vices'.[3] Byreddy Sathyanarayana Reddy, who was in the PWG since its inception and had organised the *dalams* in Khammam district, was also expelled when he questioned the ouster of Sathyamurthy. Thereafter Kondapalli Seetharamaiah became the undisputed leader of the People's War Group.

Seetharamaiah took pains to organise the front organisations of the PWG . These were the Radical Students Union (RSU), Radical Youth League (RYL), Rythu Coolie Sangham (RCS), Mazdoor Kisan Sangathan and Mahila Sravanthi. Besides, Singareni Karmika Samakhya was the Trade Union front and Jana Natya Mandali the cultural front of the party. Thus strengthened, the People's War Group embarked on a comprehensive course of action, the salient features of which were:

- redistribution of land,
- enforcing payment of minimum wages to the farm labour,
- imposing taxes and penalties,
- holding people's courts,
- destroying government property,
- kidnapping government functionaries,
- attacking policemen, and
- enforcing a social code.

The PWG is believed to have redistributed nearly half a million acres of land across Andhra Pradesh. The modus operandi was to occupy forcibly the excess land of big land-owners and give them away to the landless or to the labourers working for the landlord. As per the state government's own admission(counter affidavit 68/82 filed by the state against the Naxalites), the radicals had forcibly occupied and re-distributed 80,000 acres of agricultural land and 1,20,000 acres of forest land. These figures do not include the large number of cases which were not reported to the police for fear of reprisals by the PWG. This forced agrarian justice brought about a sea-change in the feudal system prevailing in the Telengana districts. The party activists also insisted on a hike in the daily minimum wages from Rs.15 to Rs. 25 and the annual fee for *jeetagadu* (year-long labour) from Rs. 2000 to Rs. 4000.[4] The poorer sections were particularly happy at these two measures. They found that what the politicians had been talking about and the government promising year after year could be translated into a reality only with the intervention of the Naxalites. *Gorakala doras* (Lord of the Bushes) is how the Naxalites came to be known in the interior forest areas.

Potturi Venkateswara Rao, the Editor of *Andhra Prabha*, commented as follows on PWG's grip over the Telengana districts:

> "...the PWG practically runs a 'parallel government' in Karimnagar, Warangal and Adilabad districts. It collects 'taxes and penalties' from forest and excise contractors, rich landlords and businessmen. It receives complaints from the public, conducts enquiries and investigations, holds people's courts, pronounces judgements, and awards and administers punishments."[5]

The Naxalites caused extensive damage to government property. On Oct 5, 1987, about 60 Naxalites belonging to the PWG attacked a goods train near the coal town of Ramagundam in Karimnagar district. On March 1, 1988, they set fire to Sirpur-Kagaznagar railway station; they also poured petrol on the Assistant Station Master when he refused to leave the station but no harm was caused to him. Burning of government buses was a common occurrence, the consolation being that the passengers were invariably asked to get down before the vehicle was set on fire. Destruction was on a particularly large scale if and when an important Naxalite leader was killed. Daggu Rayalingu, an important functionary of the PWG, was killed in an encounter on May 11, 1988 in Warangal. The Naxalites, in retaliation, damaged two railway stations, a telephone exchange, a microwave station, and indulged in acts of arson on two *mandal* revenue offices, many government buildings, particularly *beedi* leaf godowns and State Road Transport Corporation buses.

Kidnappings to secure the release of its own cadres was frequently resorted to by the PWG activists. The *cause celebre* was the kidnapping of six IAS Officers including a Principal Secretary of the state government and Collector of East Godavari district on December 27, 1987 while they were returning from a tribal welfare meeting at Pulimatu in the district. Their jeeps were stopped by ten gun-wielding guerillas, including three women, near Gurthedu, an interior village. The PWG demanded the release of eight jailed Naxalites. There was quite a commotion. Commandos were airlifted from Delhi. The state government however decided to play safe and the eight Naxalites in Rajahmundry jail were released. The PWG got tremendous propaganda mileage out of the incident. Mandal Praja Parishad (MPP) presidents were also kidnapped. The elected representatives of the Telugu Desam were particularly targeted. The gunning down of Daggupati Chenchuramaiah, father of Venkateswara Rao, former Minister and son-in-law of Chief Minister N. T. Rama Rao, in a village in Prakasam district stunned the Telugu Desam Party. There was a time when most of the MPP Presidents, MLAs and MPs of Adilabad, Karimnagar and Warangal districts migrated from their native villages to the cities or started living *in cognito* with relatives in far-off places.

Policemen were killed ostensibly to counter the state repression. Another objective was possibly to take away their weapons and ammunition to build up their own arsenal. In November 1986, the PWG cadres killed a Deputy Superintendent of Police and a circle inspector. Soon after, the State Committee issued a statement explaining its action:

> "The Andhra Pradesh Government has mounted repression on a large scale for the past few years in order to destroy the peasant movement launched by revolutionaries. The NTR Government has waged an undeclared war on these revolutionaries and is encouraging the police officers to kill the revolutionaries in the so-called encounters. They have killed 70 revolutionaries during the past two years. So, the situation has arisen when the revolutionaries have to protect themselves and to mount counter-action. It is as part

110

of this strategy that a DSP and a Circle Inspector were killed in Karimnagar district."[6]

The statement further said that the north Telengana districts and the adjoining forest areas had become a vast police camp where a "fascist rule" was prevailing. In 1987 there were two major incidents involving killings of policemen. On July 29, six constables were gunned down in a forest near Doragadda on the borders of East Godavari-Visakhapatnam districts. On August 18, a group of ten policemen, two sub-inspectors, one head constable and seven constables, were shot down in the Alampalli forest of Adilabad district. Another policeman was killed in a Naxalite raid on an armoury on October 8 in Karimnagar district. Killing of policemen had indeed touched a peak in 1987 as the following table would show:[7]

Year	District	No. of Policemen killed	Total	Rank
1984	Hyderabad	1	2	2 Constables
	Visakhapatnam	1		
1985	Karimnagar	3	6	3 Sub-Inspectors
	Adilabad	1		3 Constables
	Warangal	2		
1986	Nizamabad	1	4	1 Dy. Supdt of Police
	Warangal	2		1 Circle Inspector
	Karimnagar	1		2 Constables
1987	Visakhapatnam (Rural)	11	25	1 Circle Inspector
	Adilabad	10		2 Sub-Inspectors
	Warangal	2		5 Constables
	Nizamabad	1		17 Constables
	Karimnagar	1		

The police informers also got a ham-handed treatment. Their hands or legs were amputated. It is estimated that about 80 persons had their limbs severed in 1987 alone for assisting the administration.

The PWG gained a measure of popularity when it enforced a social

111

code, placing a ban on the consumption of alcohol and getting the liquor shops forcibly closed. The state government had been pursuing a liberal licencing policy with an eye on excise revenue. This had turned Andhra Pradesh into a "paradise of dipsomaniacs." The smallest towns were dotted with shops selling India made foreign liquor (IMFL) while country liquor was freely available in polythene sachets. The ban had the desired effect and a large number of liquor vendors closed their shops. Those who did not, had to suffer the wrath of the PWG. The Naxalites set ablaze an arrack depot on October 13,1990 in Mulkanur in Karimnagar district. Two bar owners who defied the ban were beaten black and blue. In Nizamabad district, the Naxalites kidnapped three arrack sales agents. The Naxalites also sabotaged the excise auctions by warning the bidders to desist from participating in them. As a result, the entire coal belt stretching from Godavari Khani to Mancherial drew a blank in the arrack auctions. The PWG also carried out a campaign against gambling and prostitution. They put up wall posters at many places in Telengana to highlight the evils of gambling. They also took steps to prevent prostitution in the red light area of Vangapadu near Warangal.

The revolutionary writers greatly helped in preparing the environment in which the Naxalite ideology found ready acceptance. The moving spirit of the Jana Natya Mandali, the cultural front of the PWG, was Gummadi Vittal Rao, better known as Gaddar. He became a balladeer after an aborted engineering career and fought the establishment with the power of his songs. The songs were simple and yet touching. One popular song addressed the untouchables, another the factory workers. *Jeepi Vattandi Ra Randira* (The jeeps are here again) was about the politician's routine begging for votes. The wandering minstrel's revolutionary songs were popular all over the state. Gaddar become something of a legend. It is said that once Gaddar sang "they feel blood rushing to their head, pride welling in their hearts and anger rising in their breasts."[8] Gaddar was jailed during the Emergency and, on release, again arrested in the Ramnagram conspiracy case. The Telugu Desam government also frowned at him. Gaddar therefore went underground in 1985 and re-surfaced in early 1990 only.

The PWG fought virtually a running battle with the state government during the Telugu Desam rule. It is interesting to recall that N. T. Rama Rao, while campaigning in 1983, had held the Naxalites as *Desabhaktulu* (patriots) but the compulsions of office forced him to take a tough line. The Naxalites never forgave him for what they considered was a *volte face* and embarrassed him repeatedly by making different demands from time to time like declaring the whereabouts of missing Naxalites, instituting a probe into the disappearance of Naxalites, removing the State Home Minister, instructions not to demolish the memorial *stupas*, release of prisoners etc. In November 1989, Chenna Reddy again assumed office as Chief Minister of the state. He pursued a very liberal policy to start with. It had a three-pronged strategy: freeing all the Naxalite prisoners who had undergone long spells of incarceration without trial or conviction, allowing freedom to the extremists to hold public meetings, and restraining the police from interfering with legitimate activities of all shades of Naxalites. At the same time, the government launched a Remote Areas Development Programme to wean the tribals away from extremist influence. The approach looked promising and it was hoped that the Naxalites would surrender and join the mainstream. Unfortunately the hopes were belied. The Naxalites took advantage of the soft approach and exploited it to swell their ranks and enhance their fire-power. They went on an extortion spree, collecting huge amounts from traders. In one instance, the traders of Nizamabad town were made to cough out Rs. 15 lacs to the PWG in April 1990. Kidnappings of course came down because there seemed to be no need to use that weapon. The state government had already released nearly 200 Naxalites detained under the various laws. The Naxalites also organised Praja Courts to dispense instant justice. As recorded by K.Srinivas Reddy, "the people's court became the main instrument not only for solving the economic problems of the exploited classes, but also to deal with legal matters, family disputes, corruption in the administration and dowry harassment cases".[9] The general impression was that the Naxalites were running a 'parallel government' in the areas under their influence. The Chief Minister was severely criticised not only by the Opposition but also by the dissident Congressmen. Chenna Reddy thereupon decided to resume the hard line.

The Naxalite violence in Andhra Pradesh, however, showed no

signs of abatement. There was a steady upward trend as the following figures illustrate:

Year	Incidents	Killed
1981	53	10
1982	98	18
1983	172	17
1984	306	30
1985	308	30
1986	161	25
1987	252	63
1988	453	59
1989	456	84
1990	735	94

An incident involving the killing of seven policemen by the Naxalites in Adilabad district on February 1,1989 marked a distinct upgradation in the weaponry and destructive skills of the PWG. They used AK-47 assault rifles for the first time and also remote-controlled land mines to blow up the police jeep. After the carnage, they decamped with two sten guns, one self-loading rifle, three .303 rifles and one .38 revolver. Ramamohan Rao, the DGP Andhra, when questioned about the Andhra Naxalites getting assault rifles from Punjab, replied: "It cannot be ruled out but we are sure about their connections with the LTTE." It is estimated that the PWG managed to acquire 50 to 60 AK-47 rifles, mostly from the LTTE.

There were other Naxalite groups also active in Andhra Pradesh during the period but they were no match to the PWG in terms of fire-power or the quantum of violence it unleashed. These groups were CPI (ML) Anti-Lin Biao faction, CPI (ML) C. P. Reddy group and the COC (ML) Party Unity. Those who shunned violence included the COI (ML) and the PCC CPI (ML) Santosh Rana group.

In due course, the People's War Group spread its organisational network to the coastal and Rayalaseema districts in the state. It extended its tentacles to the adjoining areas of Maharashtra, Madhya Pradesh and Orissa and made a dent even in the bordering districts of Karnataka and certain pockets of Tamil Nadu. Violence touched a peak in 1991. There were incidents of attacks on government property including vital installations like railway stations and telephone exchanges and kidnappings of politicians and officials. Police and para military forces personnel were particularly targeted. The PWG's taking on the Border Security Force showed their supreme self-confidence. On August 29, 1992, in a mine blast, they killed seven BSF personnel including a Deputy Commandant travelling in a jeep in Karimnagar district. On September 24, 1992, in a still more devastating mine blast, the PWG killed 13 BSF personnel in Warangal district. The BSF, in fact, suffered twenty-three casualties in 1992 and five in 1993.

The People's War Group nevertheless suffered major setbacks in 1992, partly because of internal dissensions within the party and partly because well organised counter-insurgency operations were undertaken by the State Police assisted by the Central para military forces. There was split in the party with Kondapally Seetharamaiah being replaced by Mupalla Laxmana Rao Ganapathy as General Secretary. The differences between them surfaced prominently at the Central Organising Committee meeting in August 1991 and came to a head at the Party Plenum in October 1991. The State Government's sustained pressure also took its toll. The People's War Group and its six front organisations were banned on May 20, 1992. Operations by the security forces resulted in as many as 248 Naxalites being liquidated and 3,434 party activists being arrested in 1992. The police also made a large haul of illicit firearms. The arrest of Kondapally Seetharamaiah and other important leaders added to the discomfiture of the PWG. There was considerable demoralisation among the ranks and about 8,500 of them surrendered before the authorities. Naxalite violence declined from 1230 in 1991 to 675 in 1992. It is however significant that murders did not show any appreciable fall, their numbers coming down from 233 in 1991 to 212 only in 1992.

The PWG's capacity for violence is not to be under-estimated. In January 1993, following the killing of two of its important leaders, Gundaboyina Anjaiah, Secretary Warangal District Committee and Donthe Markandeya, Secretary North Telengana Regional Committee, the PWG unleashed a wave of violence in the state. They killed K.S. Vyas, DIG Police, who had earlier worked with the anti-Naxalite unit, on January 27; kidnapped a Congress (I) MLA and seven state government officials including an IAS officer. In the Telengana area, the PWG cadres blasted the house of a state minister in Madanpally village of Warangal district, burnt state transport buses and set fire to a number of government buildings, railway stations and telephone exchanges, particularly in Warangal and Nizamabad districts. In October 1993, the killing of PWG Provincial Committee Secretary, P. Anjaiah, in an encounter in Warangal district again led to the party cadres going on rampage. Buses were burnt and there were blasts at government buildings including railway stations. On November 14, 1993, the PWG struck with a land-mine blast in Mehboobnagar district, killing nine policemen including the young Superintendent of Police. The PWG was responsible for 589 acts of violence during the year 1993 and these included 159 persons killed, 37 of them being policemen. The State Police also liquidated 141 Naxalites during the year. With all the buffetings it has received from the State government and the Central para military forces, the PWG still has good organisational strength, considerable fire-power and a network spread all over the Dandakaranya region comprising the tribal areas of Andhra Pradesh, Madhya Pradesh, Maharashtra and Orissa.

Madhya Pradesh

The tribal district of Bastar was a sleepy forest outpost until the Naxalites from Andhra Pradesh spilled over into the region. The tribals, cut off from civilization, were used to a life of deprivation. If the teacher played truant, the tribals accepted it quietly. If the doctor did not turn up, there was no protest. It is in this kind of atmosphere that the Naxalites stepped in. They caught hold of the teacher and forced him to take classes. The doctor was threatened and he started attending to the patients. This gave credibility to the Naxalites and the tribals looked at them with awe and respect. The People's Union for Civil Liberties, in an illuminating report, painted the picture of Bastar in the following words:

> "...a lopsided socio-economic development of the district, caused by indirect exploitation through environmental destruction and direct exploitation through cheating and duping, has provided an ideal setting for the Naxalites to take root in the area. They probably

understood the tribal psychology better and with their idealism, free of corruption or any other vested interest, could easily win the confidence of the simple tribals. For instance they supported the illegal encroachment of forest land and organised some campaigns of encroachment themselves; they repeatedly brought to the fore the issue of tanks and the need to maintain them in a systematic manner for irrigation; they openly opposed the Bodhghat project; they punished corrupt officials, they made the tendu leaf contractors increase the wage rates; and they held health and education programmes among tribals. All these they conducted through their front organisation, Adivasi Kisan Mazdoor Sanghatan (AKMS), which carried out legal activities like demonstrations and agitations."[10]

Initially the Naxalites were active only in South Bastar but gradually they spread their influence to North Bastar as well. There were eight *dalams* operating in the district, each having a membership of 10 to 12 persons. There were stray incidents of violence in the nature of threatening a Block Development Officer who harassed the teachers, beating up a Forest Ranger who paid low wages to the forest workers or making an errant Constable crawl before the village assembly to seek pardon for his misdeeds. The forest contractors were compelled to increase the rate of tendu leaf collections from Rs. 4 to Rs. 25 over a period of eight years in the eighties. The Naxalites also fought for tribal rights like allowing them to graze their cattle, permission to fell trees according to their need and hunting small game in the forests. Bandh calls were given on these issues from time to time. One such call was on April 20, 1990 to demand raise in the daily wages of forest labourers. The Naxalite movement subsequently spread over to Balaghat and Rajnandgaon districts also. In 1990 there were 62 incidents of Naxalite violence. These increased to 89 in 1991, Bastar accounting for 71 incidents, Balaghat 15 and Rajnandgaon 3.

The Naxalites in Bastar have been expressing their violent opposition to the parliamentary process. In the 1990 assembly poll, they burnt alive a platoon commander and murdered a sub-inspector and a jeep driver. In the 1991 Lok Sabha election, eight members of a polling party including six policemen were killed in a blast. On November

28, 1993, ten jawans of the Central Reserve Police Force were killed and a state police constable seriously injured in a powerful land-mine blast in the Naxalite dominated area of Narayanpur in Bastar district when they were returning after conclusion of the second phase of polling. The Naxalites had given a call for boycotting the elections and threatened to chop off the index fingers of villagers who exercised their franchise.

The state government has lately been showing greater sensitivity to the problems of Bastar tribals. Replying to the debate on budgetary demands related to the home and general administration department in the state assembly on April 19, 1994, Digvijay Singh, Chief Minister, said that it was his firm belief that the Naxalite problem could not be solved by mere policing. "It is a social, economic and political problem which needs to be tackled on all these fronts." A package was also announced to uplift the tribals.

Maharashtra

Gadchiroli in Maharashtra is largely inhabited by tribals. Its population of 7.87 lakhs has 38.7 per cent tribals. Out of the total of 15,434 sq. kms, jungle spreads over 10,495 sq. kms. The entire life and culture of the tribals revolves around the forest and yet, tragically, the tribals were progressively denied access to the forest through a myopic interpretation of the rules. The tribals cultivating a particular piece of land for years were evicted by the Forest Department under the Forest Conservation Act, 1980. The forest officials' contention was that this land came under the forest zone and as such was the property of the Forest Department. The Naxalites exhorted the tribals to stay on and continue with cultivation, promising them protection from any action by the Forest Department. Naturally, they were looked upon as 'messiah'.

There were indications that these Naxalites had received weapons from outside. A statement to this effect was made by Sharad Pawar, Chief Minister, on July 16,1988 when he disclosed that weapons were being pumped into Chandrapur and Gadchiroli areas which were infested with Naxalites. The Chief Minister admitted that the tribals needed to be tackled on both "social and administrative" levels.[11]

The Commissioner for Scheduled Castes and Scheduled Tribes has recorded an interesting encounter which he had during his visit to Gadchiroli in 1989:

"I was going in a jeep. I met a tribal on the way whom I gave lift in the jeep. In the course of conversation with him about the Naxals, whom the people here call Dada, I asked him: 'How are the Dadas?' He said there is at least one change after the coming of Dadas—the government atrocities are over, now the police or the guard cannot harass us."[12]

There were 113 incidents of Naxalite violence in 1990 with 16 deaths. The number of incidents came down to 96 in 1991 but the number of deaths shot up to 30. There was a particularly disastrous incident on November 12, 1991 in Etapalli tehsil of Gadchiroli district when 10 SRPF personnel were killed and 13 other policemen injured in a land-mine explosion.

The PWG have attained a high level of sophistication in the matter of using improvised explosive devices. They appear to have been trained in this art by the LTTE.

6.2 THE 'NEW LEFT' IN BIHAR

Roi roi ke kaheli Sudama se Bahuriya,
dinwa patar bhaele,
khaike sattua neikhe
raheke jhopriya neikhe,
dinwa patar bhaele
gorwaye juta neikhe
dinwa patar bhaele.

Crying, the woman tells Sudama,
The days are lean.
No *sattu* to eat
No hut to live in
The days are lean.
No shoes on our feet
The days are lean.
　　　　　　—A Musahar Poem

The state in Bihar can be said to have 'withered away,' though not in the Marxist sense of the term. There is almost complete breakdown of authority. Political chicanery, economic bankruptcy, social upheaval, and cultural degeneration sum up the overall situation. Arvind.N. Das has described the state's dismal picture in the following words:

"Bihar's economy has been at a standstill for decades. While the immense mineral and manpower resources have been used by other parts of India to climb up the development ladder, its own progress has been hindered. The blatantly unfair system of freight equalization; the discriminatory nature of public and private investments; the Green Revolution bypassing the state principally on account of non-implementation of land reforms; the adverse

120

deposit-credit ratios imposed by the banking system; the gross neglect of the state's physical infrastructure; the wilful subversion of whatever traditional or institutional social security system existed there—all these have pushed the people into poverty, the economy into backwardness, the society into violence and the culture into despair."[1]

It was but natural that the resentment of the oppressed sections in this environment should find an outlet—and this it did in the emergence of a 'New Left' which manifested itself in the form of three Naxalite groups in the beginning of 1980, viz the (i) Maoist Communist Centre, (ii) CPI (ML) Anti-Lin Biao Group and (iii) CPI (ML) Party Unity.

As early as May 1982, the Bihar Government in its *Notes on Extremist Activities-Affected Areas* reported that as many as 47 out of a total of 857 blocks spread over 14 districts were affected by the Communist extremist movement. In a research paper published in the *Economic and Political Weekly*, Professor Pradhan H. Prasad reproduced a table which showed that 10.28 per cent of the villages, 8.23 per cent of the population, 7.24 per cent of the area, 9.46 per cent of the net sown area and 11.98 per cent of the gross sown area had been affected by Communist extremist movement by 1982. Subsequently, "the movement has grown enormously in the face of the corrupt, casteist and incompetent administration of Bihar and today touches every aspect of the social life of the state."[2]

Maoist Communist Centre (MCC)

When the CPI (ML) was formed after the dissolution of the All India Coordination Committee of Communist Revolutionaries and the merger of several Maoist groups, one Naxalite group, Dakshin Desh, retained its distinct entity ('Dakshin' because India is at the south of Himalayas; China was considered Uttar Desh). Amulya Sen and Kanai Chatterjee were its leaders. They considered mass mobilisation a pre-requisite to any armed action. The Dakshin Desh Group chose Jangal Mahal area of Burdwan district as its area of operation. The region has sizeable tribal and scheduled caste population and the terrain

121

is full of forests—an ideal combination for launching a Maoist struggle. The socio-economic condition of people made them vulnerable to Maoist ideology. Agricultural land was inadequate, irrigation facilities virtually non-existent and the wage rates dismally low. The landlords generally belonged to the upper castes while the scheduled castes and tribes were mostly share-croppers or worked as landless labour.

The party organised propaganda and militia squads, whose main function was to politicise the peasantry and recruit new cadres and professional revolutionaries. These squads visited the villages after sunset when the peasants and other agricultural workers were back from their fields. At day-break they would disappear into the jungles. A number of party workers were drawn from Calcutta and its suburbs. As such they came to be known as *Banbabus* or gentlemen living in the forests. It is estimated that by 1973 the party had as many as 37 militia and propagands squads with 106 members.[3] These squads organised actions like looting of foodgrains, killing of class enemies and snatching of arms. Those killed included oppressive landowners, police informers and some who had organised resistance against the Maoists. The activities of the group remained confined to Jangal Mahal area till 1976. The party could not sustain the faith of the peasantry and its hold over the area gradually dissipated. In due course, it spilled over to the adjoining areas of Bihar. Kanai Chatterjee himself toured the Aurangabad and Gaya districts and formed an apex body known as Bengal-Bihar Special Area Committee. The group was re-named as the Maoist Communist Centre in 1975. Kanai's death in 1982 was followed by factional disputes. The new leader, Sivenji, fell out with his deputy, Ramadhar Singh, over the policy of individual annihilations. Ramadhar Singh thereupon left the MCC and joined the Kanu Sanyal faction of the CPI (ML). In the latter half of eighties, Pramod Mishra and Sanjay Dusadh emerged as the formidable leaders of the MCC.

The organisational network of the MCC gradually spread over the Central Bihar districts. The party recruited 500 whole-timers and more than 10,000 members. Its front organisation are the Krantikari Kisan Committee, Jana Suraksha Sangharsh Manch, Krantikari Budhijeevi Sangh and Krantikari Chhatra League. The party also built up an armed wing known as the Lal Raksha Dal and managed to stockpile about seven to eight hundred firearms of different description including a couple of AK-47 rifles.

Thus reinforced and well equipped, the MCC cadres embarked on a course of gruesome violence. They killed eleven Rajputs, five of them women, in village Darmia, district Aurangabad on October 7, 1986. This was followed by the massacre in Baghaura and Dalelchack villages, also of district Aurangabad, on May 29, 1987. Here, "the scale of killing, magnitude of brutality, the audacity of attack all had a new dismension."[4] The Yadav activists of the MCC slaughtered 42 Rajputs of the two villages. The womenfolk were made to place their necks on an improvised chopping block and beheaded with countrymade axes. The menfolk were either shot or had their throats slit. After the carnage, the mob torched the Rajput houses and threw the bodies into the fire. The flames could be seen for miles around but there was no succour. It would be difficult to say that the incident was motivated by any Maoist ideology to attack the class enemies. On the contrary, it would appear that the Yadav followers of the MCC were actuated by the savage instinct to settle their scores with the Rajputs. As brought out by Dr. Bindeshwar Pathak in his book *Rural Violence in Bihar*, the incident had its genesis in the Rajput farmer Kedar Singh being done to death in village Chechani, which is dominated by Yadavs, on April 18, 1987. Within hours, the Rajput supporters of Kedar Singh arrived and they killed eight Yadavs in retaliation. The slaughter at Baghaura-Dalelchack was in the chain of vendetta killings with the MCC playing the role of "hired killers". The leftists are however not willing to separate the class and caste conflicts and justify overlapping of the two. As Sumitra Jain says:

"Although both caste and class cannot be ignored while examining the incidents of this kind—caste prejudices are closely intertwined with violence in Bihar—it is difficult to separate the caste factor from economic reality.
The killings in Dalelchack and Baghaura, where the upper caste Rajputs were killed by the backwards through influential Yadavs, perhaps gives the impression that it was solely a case of caste vendetta. But the MCC (Maoist Communist Centre) indictment that described the incident as a revolutionary step against the

123

oppressive feudal forces gives the carnage a class colour. Indeed the distinction between caste and class is not very clear and they often overlap."[5]

The killings in Bara village of Gaya district on February 12, 1992 was another sordid landmark in the macabre class-cum-caste conflicts in Bihar. Here, the marauders, in a four hour orgy, hacked 37 members of the land-owning Bhumihar families. As narrated by the *Hindustan Times* correspondent:

"They called the youths and aged male persons to accompany them to a nearby place. Once they were herded together near an adjoining canal their throats were slit open one after another and the whole place bore a tell-tale testimony to the gruesome incident with patches of the blood presenting a devastating sight."

This incident also, according to Dr. Pathak, was a fall out of the un-declared war between the Savarna Liberation Front and the left extremist groups. It had nothing to do with agrarian unrest. These incidents earned a notoriety for the MCC. The profile of major incidents of violence perpetrated by the MCC has been as follows:[6]

Year	District	Killed by MCC
1986 (Sep)	Aurangabad	11 Rajputs
1987 (May)	Aurangabad	42 Rajputs
1991 (Jan)	Gaya	2 Policemen
1991 (Mar)	Gaya	5 Muslims
1991 (May)	Gaya	1 BJP MP
1991 (Dec)	Gaya	3 Bhumihars
1992 (Feb)	Gaya	37 Bhumihars
1992 (Sep)	Chatra	1 Policeman
1992 (Sep)	Gaya	5 MCC Rebels
1993 (Jan)	Gaya	3 Yadavs

Thus what had begun as a fight for social and economic justice has degenerated into a caste conflict with a veneer of class struggle. The polarisation on caste and class lines has led to a mushroom growth of Senas in Bihar. The outfits defending the interests of the landlords and the upper castes are (i) The Bhumi Sena comprising mainly the Kurmis, (ii) The Lorik Sena consisting predominantly of Yadavs, (iii) The Brahmarishi Sena having a following mostly of Bhumihars and (iv) The Kuer Sena which has a largely Rajput following. On the other hand, there are (a) The Lal Raksha Dal of the Maoist Communist Centre, (b) The Lal Sena of the Anti-Lin Biao faction, and (c) The Mazdoor Kisan Sangram Samiti owing allegiance to the Unity Committee of the CPI (ML). The proliferation of these Senas has made the rural environment highly combustible. In Bihar, as Arun Sinha says, "the major feature of social as well as political life is the prevalance of the language of force." The classes and the castes are now talking in this idiom.

The MCC has also been running virtually a parallel judicial system in certain pockets. These are described as *Jana Adalat* or People's Court. The holding of such an *adalat* in village Sanjivanbigha of Gaya district has been described by Farzand Ahmed in *India Today* in the following words:

"Silence descends as Laxman, the area commander of the MCC, a sinister figure with his face covered, appears. The two accused, with their hands tied behind their backs, are brought in. Laxman launches into his ideological monologue: 'In today's system the toiling masses work hard but don't get anything to eat. On the other hand, these bastard thieves lift goats and diesel'. He then asks the villagers to select five judges. The five-judge bench hears the charges and announces its verdict-five *lathi* blows and five slaps each by children publicly. The verdict, confirmed by the people by a voice vote is quickly executed, accompanied by the requisite slogan *'Naxalbari ek hi rasta'* (Naxalism is the only way out)."

The MCC justice has a ruthless face also. There are instances when, at the end of hearing, the self-styled judge gives a cryptic verdict: *Cheh inch chota kar do* (shorten the accused by six inches). The guilty person, in other words, is to be beheaded. Some landlords and local bullies have met this fate. The MCC violence touched a peak in 1990. There were a total of 167 incidents in which 51 lives were lost.

There have been internecine conflicts between the MCC and the other two Naxalite groups over spheres of influence. The latest incident involved the killing of five CPI (ML) Liberation Group workers in the twin villages of Uttara and Laari in district Jehanabad by the MCC on April 4, 1994. This led to Vinod Mishra damning the MCC as a *Madhya-yugin katilon ka kendra*. It is basically a rivalry for the *numero uno* slot. Ideologically, the MCC is opposed to the CPI (ML) Anti-Lin Biao faction which is considered revisionist. It has better compatibility with CPI (ML) Party Unity in the sense that both subscribe to the doctrine of armed revolution. MCC's closest affinity however is with the People's War Group. One reason for this could be that there is no territorial conflict between them. Towards the end of 1988, the Maoist Communist Centre and the People's War Group issued a joint appeal to enlist support for their objective of raising armed units and establishing struggle areas. Referring to the Naxalite activities in Bihar, the document said that their effort was to secure land for the tillers and to annex all political rights for revolutionary peasant committees. Armed peasants, it was said, had shaken the private armies maintained by landlords and were snatching arms from them and others. The pamphlet further claimed that the revolutionary peasant committees had re-distributed about 3,200 hectares of land owned by landlords among the landless and that resources like bullocks, fertilisers, ploughs and seeds "snatched" from the landlords were being utilised by the peasantry.[7]

CPI (ML) Anti-Lin Biao/Liberation Group

The Anti-Lin Biao or the Liberation Group (named after the party mouthpiece) believed that Charu Mazumdar had, towards the end, modified his formulations and accepted the need and importance of mass mobilisation and mass organisations. They endorsed the official Chinese version that Lin was guilty of 'left deviation' and had attempted to murder Mao.

Vinod Mishra is the leader of the Anti-Lin Biao Group. Born in Kanpur, Mishra studied at the Regional Engineering College, Durgapur in West Bengal. However, before he could complete the course, he became a member of the CPI (ML) in 1969. After Charu Mazumdar's death, he moved to Bihar and, in December 1973, formed the CPI (ML) Anti-Lin Biao Group. It struck roots in Bhojpur and soon spread to Rohtas, Patna, Jehanabad and Nalanda districts of Central Bihar. The group has about fifty underground armed squads of five to eight persons each and an assortment of weapons which include countrymade guns, rifles and a few sten guns. In 1990, violent activities of the faction touched a high with 106 incidents in which 40 persons were killed.

The Indian People's Front is the political front of the Anti-Lin Biao group. It was started in 1982 with Nagabhushanam Patnaik as its president. The IPF put up candidates in 53 constituencies in the Assembly Elections held in 1985, but not one of them could be elected. In the 1989 elections, however, the IPF was able to send one member to the Parliament and seven to the Assembly. The success at the hustings is attributed to a change in the strategy which was announced at a massive rally organised by the IPF at Gandhi Maidan, Patna on March 10, 1989. Vinod Mishra, who had been underground hitherto, made a public speech and declared that the Liberation Group fully supported the principles and the election strategies of the IPF. Nagabhushanam Patnaik, President of the IPF, described the coming together of the Front and Liberation Group on a common platform as "historic" and said that they would jointly work to "transform the society at all levels." It appears that the Anti-Lin Biao Group willy-nilly came to the conclusion that the forty year old Congress hegemony had ended, that the state was no longer as oppressive as it used to be, that people in general and particularly those under the IPF umbrella were more conscious of their rights, and that the Marxist-Leninist aim would be achieved only by a party which could demonstrate its mass base in the elections. It was some kind of a 'glasnost' orientation to the original Naxalite line.

The IPF held a massive rally at Delhi on Oct 8, 1990 which was remarkable for the elan and discipline of its participants. The rally was particularly aimed at fighting communalism. It expressed "its deep concern over the increasing menace of communalism," criticised the Congress for "satisfying vested interests" and the Janata Dal for trying "to capitalise on the minority vote bank." It is significant that even though the party draws its support largely from agricultural labour and poor peasants, many of whom are *dalits*, it nevertheless assailed the "*dalitism*" of Kanshi Ram's Bahujan Samaj Party and said that "the neo-Brahmins emerging from among the *dalits* are as much a target of our movement as the forwardised backwards." The party appeared unfazed by the decline in the fortunes of Communism in the West. "Regardless of whatever may be happening in Eastern Europe and Soviet Union, in our country the Left Movement definitely has a very bright future," it said. Nagabhushanam Patnaik made it abundantly clear that the IPF was against any form of secessionism, terrorism and religious fundamentalism.[8]

The Liberation Group has meanwhile been getting restive to come out in the open. The Party Congress held in Calcutta in December 1992 resolved that henceforth it would function as a political outfit. It was stated that "the party does not rule out the possibility that under a set of exceptional national and international circumstances, the balance of social and political forces may even permit relatively peaceful transfer of central power to revolutionary forces." It was however added that the party "must prepare itself for winning the ultimate decisive victory in an armed revolution," though it admitted that the situation was not ripe for such a revolution. Nagabhushanam Patnaik rebutted the charge of 'dichotomy' and said that the party would function in the open but would at the same time be prepared face state repression. The party resolved to carry on armed struggles in areas where private armies of landlords and the police "continued to perpetrate genocide." Significantly, the party congress was attended by Madan Bhandari, General Secretary of the Communist Party of Nepal and Ms Solveig Amdal, Chairperson of the Norwegian Workers' Communist Party.[9]

At a meeting held at Patna on Feb. 26 and 27, 1994, the IPF dissolved its All-India Committee and formed a convening committee to "bring in viable changes in the party fold." The convening committee under the chairmanship of Nagabhushanam Patnaik was entrusted with holding a national conference as early as possible to invite all democratic and revolutionary organisations to form a new front. Nagabhushanam Patnaik admitted that the IPF "no longer has the status or structure of a political party"—a role which has been arrogated by the Liberation Group. How far this experiment would succeed and whether there was any real need for the swapping of roles, time alone would tell. Meanwhile, the killing of seven supporters of the IPF/Liberation Group in the Bhojpur district of Bihar on March 17, 1994 gave Vinod Mishra the opportunity to demand the resignation of Laloo Yadav. The Liberation Group organised 'Bihar Bandh' on March 22, 1994 against the killings and held a massive rally at the Gandhi Maidan in Patna.

CPI (ML) Party Unity

The COC CPI (ML) led by M. Appalasuri of Andhra and the Unity Organisation of CPI (ML) led by Bhowani Roy Chowdhury of West Bengal joined hands in 1982 to form the CPI (ML) Party Unity. This group believes in a combination of underground and overground functioning. It has however no illusions about the Parliament and is totally opposed to entering the electoral fray.

The Mazdoor Kisan Sangram Samiti, a front organisation of the party, which was formed in 1982, acquired a good following among the peasants. It was headed by Dr. Vinyan and was active in the seven districts of Central Bihar. A devout follower of Jayaprakash Narayan, he parted company with the Janata Party in 1977 after he was disillusioned with its ideology and felt that it did not offer any radical solution to the problems of agricultural workers who were exploited by the upper strata of society. Dr. Vinyan was drawn towards the Naxalite movement because he felt that it could bring about the necessary changes in the feudal socio-economic system of Bihar. The MKSS waged a relentless battle for minimum wages and achieved a good measure of success. The poor farmers, particularly the landless, were motivated to fight for their rights and many of them joined the Samiti. People's Courts were set up and Dr Vinyan settled disputes between landlords and farmers. The Arwal massacre in which 21 supporters of the Mazdoor Kisan Sangram Samiti were gunned down by the police on April 19, 1986 was however a setback to the organisation. The incident arose out of a land dispute between nine families, eight scheduled and one backward caste, on the one hand and an executive engineer, also a scheduled caste, on the other. The latter had clout with the administration, and that led to police intervention on his behalf. The state government blamed the Samiti for the carnage to cover up the administration's inept handling of the incident and banned the MKSS in August 1986. Besides, a group in the MKSS led by Arvind, a hard-core militant who was in favour of action against the administration and the landlords, branched off to form Mazdoor Kisan Mukti Manch in 1987. Dr. Vinyan's influence in the party waned thereafter.

The CPI (ML) Party Unity and its front paw, the MKSS, nevertheless made a strong impact over the poorest sections of the peasantry in Bihar. The Party Unity and its front organisations have a sizeable membership of about 30,000. They also have about 25 armed squads and their arsenal includes about 150 weapons of different description including a few sten guns. Violence by the party was highest in 1990 when 175 incidents were reported with 106 casualties.

6.3   PROFILE OF VIOLENCE

Into the jaws of Death,
Into the mouth of Hell.
        —Tennyson

The Naxalites pack considerable lethal punch even though they are splintered into diverse groups.

The total number of incidents of violence in the country during the last five years have been as follows:

	Total incidents	Deaths
1989	901	231
1990	1570	413
1991	1876	474
1992	1337	503
1993	1277	470

Violence was thus at a peak in 1991 with 1876 incidents in which 474 persons were killed. The graph came down in 1992 but, significantly, the number of deaths were higher. The graph maintained its downward trend in 1993 also, but the number of deaths remained at about the same level as in 1991.

The difference between Naxalite and terrorist killings needs to be brought out. The Naxalites generally kill carefully selected targets. This is true of terrorists also, but more often than not their shooting tends to be random and directed against civilians who may not be involved either way in the struggle. The Naxalite targeted killings, viewed from this angle, are graver and have more far-reaching implications. The fact that the Naxalites have been annihilating about 500 persons per year is adequate proof, if any is needed, of their awesome fire-power and their determination to deal ruthlessly with the class enemies.

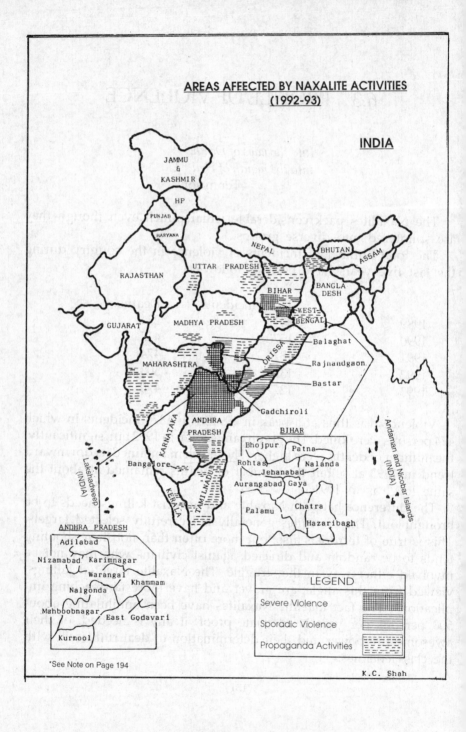

AREAS AFFECTED BY NAXALITE ACTIVITIES
(1992-93)

__INDIA__

JAMMU & KASHMIR

HP

PUNJAB

HARYANA

NEPAL

BHUTAN

ASSAM

RAJASTHAN

UTTAR PRADESH

BIHAR

BANGLA DESH

GUJARAT

MADHYA PRADESH

WEST-BENGAL

ORISSA

Balaghat

Rajnandgaon

Bastar

MAHARASHTRA

Gadchiroli

KARNATAKA

ANDHRA PRADESH

Andaman and Nicobar Islands (INDIA)

Lakshadweep (INDIA)

Bangalore

KERALA

TAMILNADU

BIHAR

Bhojpur

Patna

Rohtas

Nalanda

Jehanabad

Aurangabad

Gaya

Palamu

Chatra

Hazaribagh

ANDHRA PRADESH

Adilabad

Nizamabad

Karimnagar

Warangal

Khammam

Nalgonda

Mahboobnagar

East Godavari

Kurnool

*See Note on Page 194

LEGEND

Severe Violence

Sporadic Violence

Propaganda Activities

K.C. Shah

A comparison of Naxalite violence in 1971, 1981 and 1991 is both interesting and relevant. The period from the middle of 1970 to the middle of 1971 had witnessed the maximum Naxalite violence. It is estimated that about 4,000 incidents took place during that gory phase in which 565 lives were snuffed out. Later, with the demise of Charu Mazumdar, dissensions in the party and with several groups calling off the annihilation campaign, the quantum of violence came down and in 1981 there were only 325 incidents involving loss of 92 lives. With the formation of People's War Group in Andhra Pradesh under the leadership of Kondapally Seetharamaiah, the movement picked up momentum again and violence touched a high watermark in 1991.

State-wise, the following table gives the profile of violence during the last three years (figures in brackets indicate the number of deaths):

	1991	1992	1993
Andhra Pradesh	1230(233)	675(212)	589(159)
Bihar	415(166)	400(224)	510(250)
Madhya Pradesh	89(36)	121(36)	72(21)
Maharashtra	96(30)	72(22)	68(37)
Orissa	14(1)	32(1)	13(1)
West Bengal	12(6)	27(7)	12(2)
Other States	20(2)	10(1)	13(-)
Total	1876(474)	1337(503)	1277(470)

Andhra Pradesh and Bihar accounted for 87.68 per cent of the total incidents in the country in 1991, 80.40 percent in 1992 and 86.06 percent in 1993.

West Bengal, whence the sparks flew all over the country, is having very little Naxalite violence today. The movement would seem to have run out of steam in that state. This is to be attributed mainly to the fact that the CPM implemented the land reforms sincerely, and this has been acknowledged by the Planning Commission.

The southern states(other than AP) do not figure in the table given above. However, it must be placed on record that Naxalite activities have been noticed off and on in Tamil Nadu, Kerala and Karnataka. In Tamil Nadu, the call for a separate Tamil homeland was incorporated into the movement's ideology around the time the LTTE started clandestine activities in the state. The brain behind this was of Perunchitranar, a language zealot and a rabid advocate of scessionism. The Naxalites organised themselves into Tamil Nadu Liberation Front under the leadership of Thamizharasan. The TNLF shot into limelight in March 1987 with a blast on the Rockfort Express in which 25 passengers were killed. In November 1993, the TNLF members attacked a police station in Kullanchavadi in South Arcot district, killing a constable and injuring three others. On March 29, 1994, an extremist, Lenin, was killed in South Arcot when the bomb he was carrying accidentally exploded. Ms Jayalalitha, Chief Minister, disclosed in the Assembly that Lenin belonged to the Tamil Nadu Viduthalai Padai (Liberation Army), a Marxist-Leninist group, and that he was involved in bombing of the TV Relay Station at Kumbakonam on May 24, 1992, blasting of the rail-track in Kallagam on October 24, 1992 and also bombing of the Congress Party offices in Aathur and Kodavassal on the eve of Independence Day, 1993. The Naxalites are active mainly in South Arcot, Thanjavur and Tiruchy. The Kerala Communist Party under the leadership of K Venu has been propounding the thesis of 'nationality struggles'—that India is not a nation but a conglomeration of nationalities based on language, ethnic identity and religion. The KCP explains the struggle by the various nationalities—Sikhs, Assamese, Tamilians and others—as movements against the oppression of the dominant ruling nationality of the North. In Karnataka, Bangalore has been used as a sanctuary where Naxalites have been holding meetings, exchanging information and dumping contraband items including arms and ammunition.

The Naxalites have built up a sizeable arsenal. All the groups taken together in the country should be having about 100 assault rifles, 6,000 rifles of different calibre and 10,000 countrymade weapons of different description. It is also significant that the PWG have mastered the art of land mine explosions with the training imparted by the LTTE and have been blowing up police and paramilitary forces vehicles with abandon. In 1993 alone, the PWG used improvised explosive devices on ten occasions, seven in Andhra Pradesh, two in Maharashtra and one in Madhya Pradesh, killing a total of 47 police and paramilitary personnel and 21 civilians. Lately, the PWG caused two major land-mine explosions in Warangal and Karimnagar districts in the last week of

November 1994 to enforce its writ on the boycott of polls. Fourteen policemen, including five commandos of the Punjab Police, were killed in the process.

It may be recalled that Charu Mazumdar wanted to form a People's Liberation Army with only 60 rifles and 200 pipe-guns. Compared to that modest target, the Naxalites today have a formidable arsenal. Its implications need no emphasis.

The Government of India organised a meeting of the Chief Ministers of Andhra Pradesh, Bihar, Orissa, Maharashtra and Madhya Pradesh in New Delhi on August 3, 1991 to evolve a coordinated plan of action to combat the Naxalite violence. It was decided to constitute a joint coordination committee with representatives from different states to pursue these plans and monitor their implementation. Paramilitary units were made available to the states, who were also given the facility to train their personnel in jungle warfare under the aegis of the National Security Guard. Sophisticated weapons like AK-47 rifles were released by the Centre for the state police forces. These administrative measures have by and large had the desired effect and the sharpness of Naxalite violence has been blunted of late—except in Bihar, where the state government response has been lackadaisical.

However, it needs to be emphasised that police action by itself would never lead to a solution of the problem, whose roots go much deeper and are essentially related to the socio-economic conditions of the poor and landless farmers and the dispossesed and alienated tribals. The stress should be on tackling the basic causes. Unfortunately, this is an area where pious sentiments are expressed, elaborate plans are made, but the vested interests supported by an obliging bureaucracy frustrate the implementation of the plans. Unless that is ensured, the lava of popular resentment would continue to erupt from time to time leading to violence, bloodshed and mayhem.

7

RETROSPECT AND PROSPECT

7 RETROSPECT AND PROSPECT

Time present and time past
Are both perhaps present in time future,
And time future contained in time past.
                                    —T.S. Eliot

The Naxalite movement had its ups and downs during the last nearly twenty-seven years of its existence. Starting from Naxalbari in 1967, it rose to a crescendo in 1971 when its impact was felt in the farthest corners of the country. The sympathisers thought that "a new sun and a new moon" promised by Kanu Sanyal would now shine on the Indian skies. But the split in the party, the death of Charu Mazumdar and the joint Army-Police operations gave, what then appeared, *coup de grace* to the movement. The movement however continued to simmer and, for the next ten years, it was on a plateau. It was also the time when the basic formulations underwent a complete overhaul. Annihilation of class enemies was given up as the creed, and the Naxalite groups gradually veered round participation in the electoral process. The power of the barrel of the gun had been tested. It was time to see the power of the ballot box. Meanwhile the formation of the People's War Group in Andhra Pradesh in 1980 ushered in a new phase of heightened militancy accompanied by aggressive violence. With Andhra Pradesh as the epicentre, the movement spilled over not only to the adjoining states of Maharashtra, Madhya Pradesh and Orissa, but also to Bihar, West Bengal, Karnataka and Tamil Nadu. The Naxalite violence touched a peak in 1991, but the movement was hit hard as a result of the coordinated anti-insurgency operations undertaken in the affected states. The only exception is the state of Bihar where the *danse macabre* continues.

A Splintered Movement

The movement today is in a very fragmented state. There are about forty odd groups operating under various labels in different parts of the country. Ten of them could be considered active: these are the People's War Group, Maoist Communist Centre, CPI(ML) Liberation Group, CPI(ML) Party Unity, CPI(ML) K. Ramachandran faction, CPI(ML) Phani Bagchi Group, CPI(ML) Yatindra Kumar Group, Kerala Communist Party, CPI(ML) Red Flag and Communist Organisation of India(ML). The first four have sizeable following and are conspicuously violence-prone.

The heterogenous formations nevertheless have varying degrees of influence in no less than ten states of the Union. In Andhra Pradesh and Bihar their presence is formidable. The neighbouring states of Madhya Pradesh, Orissa, Maharashtra and West Bengal are also affected. To a lesser extent, Naxalite presence is noticed in the states of Kerala, Karnataka, Tamil Nadu and parts of Eastern UP.

Efforts at unification were made from time to time but these invariably proved abortive. The leaders differed on personal and ideological issues, though it would seem that personality clashes overshadowed and took precedence over doctrinnaire formulations. In May 1985, six Naxalite groups announced their merger and the formation of a Communist Organisation of India (Marxist-Leninist) after prolonged deliberations at Naxalbari. The six groups were the Organising Committee of the Communist Revolutionaries led by Kanu Sanyal, the CPI(ML) Kaimur Range led by Ravi Shankar, the Central Organising Committee of the CPI(ML) headed by Umadhar Singh, the Unity Centre of the Communist Revolutionaries of India(ML) of Subodh Mitra, the Indian Communist Party headed by Krishnappa of Karnataka and the Liberation Front of Sabuj Sen. Kanu Sanyal, who was elected General Secretary of the COI(ML), said that the six Marxist-Leninist groups had learnt their lessons from the past and that they would try to bring about unification of the other like-minded groups scattered all over the country. Sanyal clarified that the ultimate aim of the COI(ML) would be armed struggle against the established order and that, in pursuance of the same, the party would adopt both legal and illegal means. While repudiating the parliamentary process, Sanyal said that the COI(ML) would nevertheless "participate in elections to mobilise the masses wherever necessary."

The merger of six revolutionary group appeared *prima facie* to be a major step, but with the exception of Kanu Sanyal's group of Organising Committee of Communist Revolutionaries (OCCR), the other groups had a marginal following. The unified body, in any case, failed to make any impact and, in 1989, the party admitted that it had "failed to realise its declared objective of uniting the communist revolutionary forces" in the country. "Our unification was achieved primarily at the top. Likewise, all our problems emanate from the top. We had made known our political differences and pledged to resolve them through organised debate. The Central Committee failed to launch required debates and left important political questions undisturbed while spending much of its time splitting hairs on the differences between people's democracy and new democracy or our role in insignificant organisations," the political and organisational report said. Almost sounding a note of despair, it added: "The future path remains tortuous. Resolution of disputes among various communist revolutionary groups has indeed proved difficult."[1]

At the other end of the spectrum, the People's War Group, the Maoist Communist Centre and the CPI(ML) Party Unity decided in September 1993 to join hands to intensify the Naxalite movement in Andhra Pradesh, Bihar, Maharashtra and the other states. These parties have together constituted All India Peoples Resistance Forum, an apex body representing the constituent groups, to "build and develop powerful anti-feudal and anti-imperialist struggles." The AIPRF held a massive rally of about one lac people at the Shahid Minar Maidan in Calcutta on March 21, 1994. The participants were largely from West Bengal and Bihar but there were representatives from several other states also. Tribals with bows and arrows were conspicuous by their presence. A ten-member executive committee was formed. The fate of this coordination would need to be watched with interest as the People's War Group, the Maoist Communist Centre and the Party Unity have enough fire-power and account for the bulk of Naxalite violence in the country.

In West Bengal, at the instance of PWG, there was recently an effort to unify some of the smaller groups like the Lal Jhanda, Shanti Paul, Subir Talukdar and Dilip Banerjee group.

A fall-out of the splintered character of the movement is that it has no charismatic leader at the top. The sixties were dominated by

141

Charu Mazumdar who, with all his faults and aberrations, was able to inspire people throughout the length and breadth of the country with his brilliant, even if convoluted, formulations. In the seventies, Satyanarayan Singh occupied the centre-stage. The eighties belonged to Kondapally Seetharamaiah. In the nineties, the only person who is nearest to having an all-India stature is Vinod Mishra of the Liberation Group.

The CPI(ML) Liberation has, in fact, gradually emerged as the most important overground Naxalite formation in the country. Through its front organisations like the Bihar Pradesh Kisan Sabha, All India Coordination Committee of Trade Union, All India Students Association (AISA) and particularly the Indian People's Front(IPF), the party has embarked on an ambitious programme to have mass base all over Bihar. Vinod Mishra, General Secretary of the Liberation Group, is aiming at a federation of the left parties. "It is in the logic of things that all mainline left parties align together. That is the only alternative to the welter of political shades and opinions. The left is the third and most viable alternative," according to him. The Liberation Group is, at the same time, keeping its powder dry. As Vinod Mishra says, "We are prepared for bloody conflict. Even civil war".[2] The party is trying to make its presence felt in the south also. A rally was held at Madras on April 10, 1994 to protest against "the corrupt, dictatorial and trecherous" state government. The indications are that the Liberation Group would assimilate in its programme the sentiments and aspirations of the Dravidian people.

Even though hopelessly fragmented, the Naxalites have an awesome arsenal. Their capacity for violence remains formidable.

Support Base

The total membership of all the Naxal groups of various shades is around fifty thousand. Numerically this is a small figure for a country like India. The Naxalite cadres are drawn mostly from the oppressed and exploited farmers and tribals. The intellectual appeal of the movement however goes far beyond its actual following, and it has a large support base with lakhs of sympathisers. The Naxalite ideology has a strong gravitation for the student community—and that explains

142

IPF's success in the student union elections in Allahabad University, BHU, Kumaon University and the JNU in 1992-93. The Naxalites have a limited following among the labour class also.

The large number of civil liberties groups in the country have a soft corner for the Naxalities and espouse their cause vis-a-vis the administration. These groups have been particularly active in states like Andhra Pradesh, Delhi, Kerala and Tamil Nadu. The fact-finding committees appointed by them to investigate the encounters in which Naxalites were killed by the police have provided grist to their propaganda mills, thereby building up a climate of sympathy for the left-wing extremists. In the cultural field, the pro-extremist bodies have successfully exploited the medium of drama and poetry to propagate the Naxalite ideology. The Janakiya Samskarika Vedi in Kerala, the Jana Natya Mandali in Andhra Pradesh, the Natak Kala Kendra in the Punjab and the Nishant Natya Manch in Delhi have served revolutionary themes in attractive package.

In an effort to broaden their base, the Naxalites have been taking up the cause of minorities and ethnic groups. In the wake of demolition of the disputed structure at Ayodhya, some Naxalites raised the demand for safeguarding and guaranteeing the rights of the Muslim minority. Kanu Sanyal's COI(ML) holds the view that India is not a nation and that "a multi-national government is in power which is exploiting and oppressing the less advanced nationalities, who virtually do not enjoy any political or democratic rights."[3] Accordingly he supports independence for Jammu & Kashmir, Mizoram and Nagaland. There are also indications that the PWG and the MCC have been trying to establish links with the insurgent groups of the north-east. It is difficult to say if such theories or efforts would lead to broadening or further erosion of the Naxalite base. The Naxalite efforts to secure allies in social action groups, reformers and environmentalists is less open to question and may contribute to a more open and democratic functioning of the outfits.

Extra-territorial Links

The extra-territorial links of the movement have considerably weakened over the years. The downgrading of Mao Zedong in his own

143

country, the reforms of Deng Xiao-ping, the disintegration of the Soviet Union and the collapse of Communism in Eastern Europe have contributed to this development. An article published in the *People's Daily* in December 1984 which suggested that the writings of Marx and Lenin could not be expected to solve all the current problems caused considerable consternation among the left-wing extremists. It amounted to an attack on the Marxist-Leninist orthodoxy. The head of the three-member Chinese delegation, Jiang Guang-hua, attending the CPI Congress in March 1989, said that it was incorrect on the part of the Communist Party of China to have supported Naxalites in the past. He admitted that during the Cultural Revolution "our party and the government both were in abnormal state". So something done at that time might have been improper and incorrect. They had since changed and corrected their stand on the issue. The cumulative result of all this has been that the Naxalites are gradually settling for an indigenous methodology of class struggle and agrarian revolution, though it is essentially a slow and painful process. Marxism-Lenism is still quoted and Mao continues to be the source of inspiration. The PWG, MCC and the Party Unity, at a joint meeting held towards the end of 1993, adopted a resolution describing Mao Tse-tung Thought as "the Marxism-Leninism of the present day." They also expressed solidarity with the Peruvian Communist Party and pledged support for the unconditional release of Abimael Guzman, leader of the Shining Path, who was sentenced to life imprisonment.

The most important lesson of the Naxalite movement, as Biplab Dasgupta has appropriately said, is that "it is suicidal to adopt a particular prototype of revolution without judging its relevance to the history, culture, social and economic conditions and political realities of the country concerned."[4] The sooner the Naxalites understand this simple truth, the better it would be for them and the country. Mao himself was a staunch nationalist. In an article *The Role of the Chinese Communist Party in the National War*, Mao posed the question: "Can a Communist, who is an internationalist, at the same time be a patriot?" and answered in the following words:

"We hold that he not only can be but must be. The specific content of patriotism is determined by historical conditions... in wars of national liberation patriotism is applied internationalism."

The Naxalities are today on their own with no shoulders to lean on. The fact that the movement is continuing without any external support—a plus point which neither the Punjab terrorists nor the Kashmiri militants could claim—shows that it has acquired an inherent strength and a certain momentum of its own.

Ideological Dilution

On the ideological plane, there has been considerable dilution in the revolutionary fervour of the Naxalite groups. Most of the formations have opted for a combination of underground and overground functioning. The overground set up concentrates on mass mobilisation and even participates in the electoral process; the underground set up comprising armed squads or *dalams* annihilate class or caste enemies and, from to time, inflict blows on the state apparatus.

The important left wing extremist groups which have participated in elections include the CPI(ML) Anti-Lin Biao faction, CPI(ML) C P Reddy group, CPI(ML) S R Bhaiji group, the COI(ML) and the PCC CPI(ML) Santosh Rana group. In the assembly elections held in 1985, as many as 130 candidates belonging to various Naxalite groups took part in eight states, the majority of contestants being from Andhra Pradesh and Bihar. Only two candidates were successfully returned. In the assembly elections held in 1989, various extremist groups fielded 39 candidates for the Lok Sabha and 67 for the assembly seats. Another 117 candidates contested the state assembly elections held in 1990. The Indian People's Front (IPF) candidate from Arrah (Bihar) became the first left wing extremist Member of Parliament. C P Ramachandran and Bhaiji groups were able to capture one assembly seat each in Andhra Pradesh while the IPF won seven seats in the Bihar assembly. The Indian People's Front has put up the best show at the hustings so far. The party was however recently divested of its political role; it would henceforth function as an umbrella organisation of various political organisations to "unite the left and socialist forces" and carry forward their "extra parliamentary struggle." The political role has devolved on the Liberation Group under the leadership of Vinod Mishra.

The Naxalites argue that they are participating in the elections only to expose the "futility" of the system and are using the democratic exercise to consolidate and expand their support base. This is however only to disarm the critics who favour the unadulterated Maoist line of armed struggle. Besides, politics has such a baneful and corrupting influence on its participants that it is most unlikely that on being voted to power, if at all, any of the Naxalite groups would retain their zest for class struggle or the democratic revolution.

The People's War Group, the Maoist Comunist Centre, the Party Unity, the Kerala Communist Party and the Red Flag are totally opposed to any participation in the elections.

The ideological debate has, in fact, taken a back seat. Vinod Mishra, in an interview, said that "it is necessary that polemics be buried and each group ...concentrate on its own field of action and develop the struggles further with people's participation."[5]

Struggle Areas

Andhra Pradesh and Bihar constitute the two important Naxalite struggle areas in the country. In 1993, these two states together accounted for about eighty-six per cent of the total number of violent incidents perpetrated by Naxalites all over the country. Why is Naxalism strident in these two states? There are basically two reasons. One is that both the states have a tradition of peasant struggles. The Telengana region had rebelled against the feudal aristocracy of the Nizam in 1946. The Girijans had raised the banner of revolt in Srikakulam against feudal exploitation. Bihar similarly witnessed the uprising of Birsa Munda and the peasant movement of Swami Sahajanand Saraswati who founded the first Kisan Sabha. Secondly, both these states have a dismal record of land reforms. Whatever laws were enacted to disburse excess land among the landless in these two states were successfully circumvented by the landlords. Besides, the Green Revolution further consolidated the power of big landlords and led to the impoverishment of the small farmers and poor peasants.

The People's War Group in Andhra Pradesh has been spearheading the Naxalite movement during the last decade. It has provided the main thrust to militancy in the adjoining states also. Sustained and well cordinated counter-insurgency measures during 1991-92 have however been having a telling effect on the strength and morale of its cadres. 248 Naxalites were liquidated in 1992 and another 141 in 1993. There have been large scale surrenders as well. Nimmaluri Bhaskar Rao Malik, Provincial Committee Member, who was regarded as Rasputin of the PWG, surrendered on March 25, 1994. There are indications that, faced with these reverses, the PWG leadership is having serious misgivings about pursuing the cult of violence which, some of them feel, has been counter-productive. The documents recovered from a Naxal den in Bangalore as also the coming out of Bhaskar Rao seem to confirm this trend. It is also a fact that the Revolutionary Writers' Association(RWA), the Jana Natya Mandali (JNM) and the Andhra Pradesh Civil Liberties Committee (PCLC) have lately muted their support for the PWG. Driven almost to the wall, the Central Organising Committee of the People's War Group directed its cadres to join hands with other extremist groups and political parties to form a broad united front on major issues so that they could motivate people to take part in joint struggles. The PWG acknowledged that it could not fight the powerful forces of the government alone and that, therefore, it was necessary to enlarge their circle of friends, motivate the majority of people to revolt and encircle the "enemy" on all fronts.

In Bihar the Naxalites have been running some kind of a parallel administration over the south-central districts where they hold almost complete sway. The graph of violence continues to rise and there were 400 incidents of Naxalite violence in 1992 involving 224 killings. These figures shot upto to 510 in 1993 with 250 murders. The Maoist Communist Centre is the biggest perpetrator of Naxalite violence in the state. It has entrenched itself in Gaya, Aurangabad, Palamu, Chatra, Hazaribagh, Giridih, Dhanbad and parts of Jehanabad, Nawada and Nalanda districts. In the words of Arvind N.Das:

"Today the most striking feature of Bihar is violence. There is violence in the operations of mafias in the coal-mines. There is violence in Harijan-hunting in Bhojpur, Jehanabad, Patna and Nalanda and the massacre of poor peasants elsewhere. Violence claims the headlines when scrap-pickers are pushed to death in the Subarnarekha river in affluent Jamshedpur, or when prisoners are

147

blinded in jails. There is violence in trains, buses, streets, homes—in the very air of Bihar."[6]

The Chief Justice of Patna High Court, while sitting in a division bench on April 5, 1994, remarked that the law and order in the state had completely failed and warned the state government that the court might record a judicial finding to that effect which would have its own implications.

Comparison With Latin American Struggles

How does the Naxalite movement compare with the revolutionary struggles in Latin America which has been described as the "guerilla continent *par excellence*." There are basic differences, but it is interesting to find striking similarities also. The Latin American guerillas drew their inspiration from Che Guevara's formulations that popular forces could win war agaist an enemy, that it was not necessary to wait for a revolutionary situation to arise and that the same could be created by a revolutionary focus. This was fundamentally opposed to the teachings of Marxism-Leninism or even Maoism in which political party is the leading force and there is great emphasis on ideology and indoctrination. In Guevarist concept, the political party does not play the central role; the guerilla must be a social reformer (to distinguish him from a bandit) but the revolutionary concept is somehow taken for granted, and so is the support of the people.

There are essentially four points of similarities. The Latin American radicals, like the left-wing extremists of India, were also split into dozens of factions and hundreds of *groupuscules*. There were bitter recriminations among the Venezuelan, Peruvian and Bolivian guerillas. Very rarely did the guerillas make common cause. Thus, in February 1974, the Bolivian ELN, the Tupamaros, the Chilean MIR and the Argentinian ERP set up a Junta of Revolutionary Coordination(JCR). But generally there was disunity and internal strife. The CPI(ML) in India was plagued with internal dissensions from the very year of its birth and today the Naxalite groups in Bihar are at each others' throats. Secondly, the centre of gravity in Latin America shifted during the late sixties from the countryside to the cities. This orientation was considered necessary because the rural guerilla movements had been generally unsuccessful and, more importantly, Latin America had the fastest rate of urbanisation with a constant inflow of poor, unskilled and jobless people to the towns. Greater Buenos Aires had 45 percent of the total population of Argentina and Greater Montevideo had 46 percent of all Uruguayans. Between 1968 and 1972, hundreds of banks were looted in Brazil and Uruguay, political leaders annihilated, businessmen and foreign representatives kidnapped, and the 'enemies' executed or kept in 'people's prisons'. In India also, Charu Mazumdar's exhortation to the youth and students in 1970 had led to urban actions in Calcutta and other towns. Thirdly, the Latin American guerillas were temperamentally *golpistas*, anxious to topple the system with one big push. They did not have the patience or the perseverance for sustained efforts over a prolonged period. The only exception was the Columbian ELN under Fabio Vasquez which struggled for more than a decade. Charu Mazumdar was also anxious to achieve the liberation of India by 1975. His impatience led to Naxalite cadres giving up the concept of self-defence and plunging headlong into confrontations where their disintegration at the hands of vastly superior forces was a foregone conclusion. Fourthly, the immediate success of the Latin American guerillas, like that of their Indian counterparts, was astounding. But these were followed by setbacks and, in some cases, by total collapse. The Latin American revolutionaries were nearest to victory in Venezuela and Uruguay. The insurrection in Venezuela in the early sixties spearheaded by the MIR (Movement of the Revolutionary Left) and the Communists, who together established the FALN(Armed Forces of National Liberation) and the urban terrorist operations of the UTC (Tactical Combat Units) came quite close to success, but they had no real mass support as the election results of 1963 showed. In Uruguay, the Tupamaros (MNL) posed a formidable challenge between 1968 and 1972 and, like the PWG, frequently resorted to kidnappings. The circumstances in which Sendic, the Tupamaro leader, was arrested in 1970 were ironically similar to those of Charu Mazumdar's apprehension in 1972—there was no resistnce! In Bolivia, the revolution was overthrown by an army *putsch*, the Gautemalan revolution was destroyed by imperialist intervention, the Mexican revolution rotted by internal sloth and decay, and in Brazil 'Acao Libertadara Nacional' was suppressed with American help. The Naxalite movement was also eclipsed by 1972.

The one Latin American country where Maoist ideology has made headway is Peru. This is partly because the brutal slaughter of the Incas by the Spanish conquistadores, beginning with the murder of the Inca king Atahualpa, is a vital element of Andean memory. The racial system with whites at the top followed by people of mixed blood (the *mestizos*) and finally the Indians has kept Indian resentment alive. Besides, there is a similarity between the Chinese and Inca traditions with Chinese concepts of the *ying* and the *yang* corresponding to the Inca *hanang* and *hurin*. The Shining Path, Peru's insurgent outfit, carried out a ruthless struggle under the leadership of Abimael Guzman. It is estimated that Shining Path violence and Peruvian state's counter-violence have, since 1980, taken a toll of about 30,000 lives. At one stage, the Shining Path appeared to take over the banner of world revolution with the collapse of the Soviet bloc and with China and Cuba having turned "revisionists"—until Guzman was captured by the Peruvian security forces in September 1992.

The Naxalite struggle in India today is concerned with down to earth questions—issues relating to land, payment of fair wages, deforestation, displacement of tribals, etc—in rural areas and tribal pockets. The situations are already there and there is no need to create a revolutionary focus. The movment is sustained and fertilised by the grievances of the people, and the state apparatus with its enormous resources and formidable strength has not been able to stamp it out during the last nearly quarter century. The spirit of a people yearning for social justice and minimum economic well-being cannot be vanquished.

Resurgence in Future?

The question naturally arises: would there be a revival of Naxalite activities on an all India scale in a virulent form, the way it was in early seventies? Would the seething discontentment of those living below the poverty line and suffering from a sense of injustice, real or perceived, lead to violent outbursts? It is difficult to give a simple or direct answer to this question. It would be necessary to analyse the causal factors which gave rise to Naxalism in the late sixties before even an attempt is made to answer this ticklish question.

The origin and growth of Naxalite movement could be attributed to a complex of economic, social and political factors. The economic factors, which are not easy to define, would perhaps vary from state to state. Broadly speaking, these would include extreme poverty, glaring economic inequalities and exploitation, and persistent unemployment or underemployment. We have seen how the *bhagchasis* were exploited by the *jotedars* in Naxalbari. We have also seen how the Girijans in Srikakulam district led a miserable existence and that, in spite of legislative enactments, land was systematically alienated from tribals to the plains people. On the social plane, exploitation was as oppressive and, in certain instances, even worse. In the Telengana area, the landlords belonging to the Reddy and Velama communities—*Doras* as they were called—severely oppressed the poor farmers. A vivid picture of this kind of exploitation in Aurangabad district of Bihar is given in the following report:

"The poor peasants and landless labourers of Aurangabad district, earlier a subdivision of the old Gaya district, are still subject to actual feudal exploitation. They cannot sit on the cot before the landlords and their henchmen. They have to pay respect not only to their landlord masters but to the latter's toughs as well. Growing a moustache and wearing washed clothes or shoes are considered crimes. Physical exploitation, humiliation and assault of Harijans are routine affairs. Harijans constitute 30 per cent of the population of the district. Nearly 50 per cent of the people are landless, while 80 per cent of the land is owned by a mere 5 per cent. The present wage for a day's work is Rs. 4 or 2 to 3 kgs of usually coarse grains. But landlords cheat the labourers in paying even these wages which are less than half the prescribed minimum wages. The poor remain in debt for long periods and some for generations. So they are forced to work for landlords as bonded or attached labourers."[7]

Social and economic exploitation together constitute a highly combustible mixture. However what ignites this explosive combination is when people lose their faith in the established political processes

151

and administration, when they see that the state apparatus is hand-in-glove with vested interests, when they find that justice is not available to them through the normal processes of law which are long drawn out and much too complicated, when they feel that the representatives of the peple are busy feathering their own nests rather than looking after the interests of the people they represent. External factors catalyse the process. By late sixties, China had emerged as the leader of the world revolution. It was the role model for revolutionaries all over.

We shall have to see to what extent these factors operate in the present milieu. Let us take up the economic aspect first because it constitutes the very core of the problem. It has been estimated that approximately 360 million Indians i.e. about 43 per cent of the total population lived below the official poverty line in 1987-88 and 80 per cent of them lived in rural areas.[8] This is a staggering figure. In fact, this was the population of the country at the time of partition and it, therefore, implies that a large mass of humanity grinds a miserable existence today even after four decades of development efforts. This is to be attributed largely to the imbalance between the growth of population and the growth of economy. The government did tackle the problem of poverty and achieve a measure of success, but the results were more than offset by the population explosion. A pertinent question would be whether the incidence of poverty has declined or not as a result of the planned efforts. Here, unfortunately, we find that different economists have different perceptions depending on their own ideological background. On the one hand, we have Planning Commission estimates which show that between 1978 and 1990 the rural population below the poverty line fell absolutely from 253 million to 169 million and declined as a proportion of population from 51 per cent to 28 per cent. Urban poverty levels are estimated to have declined similarly. Montek S. Ahluwalia claims that "there was perceptible drop in the late seventies in the percentage of population living below the poverty line and this appears to have continued into the eighties."[9] On the question of inequalities, Ahluwalia is not so confident and merely says that"the distribution of income in India, as measured by the usual indicators of inequality, is among the more equal in the developing world."

On the other hand, we have a rather gloomy assessment by Jayati

Ghosh and Krishna Bharadwaj who are of the view that the official surveys do not necessarily fully capture changes in the material living standards of poorer groups. "Poverty is multi-dimensional reflecting not only an inadequate intake of foodgrain, but also the inability to obtain other essential food and clothing, a minimum level of acceptable housing, an access to basic medical and educational facilities. It is thought that the majority of Indian population has inadequate access to these basic necessities of life."[10] Ghosh and Bharadwaj further argue that the poverty scenario should be studied against the macro-economic indicators of income, employment, consumption and assets.

"The macro-economic indicators above point to the conclusion that income inequalities have increased in India. While there has been significant growth, particularly in some sectors, the benefits of this growth have not really 'trickled down' to reach the mass of the people. Rather, a significant proportion of the population appears to have been excluded from the beneficial effects of higher income levels in the aggregate, and in some cases their standards of living may even have worsened due to the greater precariousness of means of earning a livelihood. Although there have been some improvements in material conditions, there is evidence to suggest that the pattern of developemnt has been skewed in favour of the better-off sections of society, and the relatively disadvantaged have not been able to improve their position to any significant extent."[11]

A more objective and balanced assessment would be found in S D. Tendulkar, K. Sundaram and L R Jain's *Poverty in India: 1970-71 to 1988-89.* Their conclusions are:

i) Poverty in India is predominantly a rural phenomenon; nearly 75 percent of the poor belonged to the rural sector in 1987-88.
ii) The structure of poverty has by and large remained unchanged during the eighties; it was much the same in 1987-88 as in 1983.
iii) In rural areas, the worst off are rural labour households, pre-dominantly agricultural labour households, accounting for a third of the rural population.

iv) In urban areas, the worst off are the casual labour households such as construction workers, head-load workers, etc.

v) The households belonging to Scheduled Castes and Scheduled Tribes, who constitute about 30 percent of the rural population and 15 percent of the urban population, are highly over- represented in the group of poor.

vi) Rural poverty is concentrated in Central and Eastern India and in a few pockets in Western and Southern India.[12]

The above conclusions have been endorsed by the United Nations Development Programme in its study *India: Employment, Poverty and Economic Policies* (December 1993).

It is amazing that the face of poverty has just not changed in certain areas even when interest was taken at the highest level. As brought out by P. Sainath, people in Kalahandi (Orissa) continue to suffer acute hunger and parents still abandon their children because there is not enough to survive on. Even the visit of Prime Minister Rajiv Gandhi made no difference to the life of Phanas Punji who sold her fourteen year old sister-in-law Banita Punji nine years back for a mere Rs. 40, sparking off a furious national debate. The Director General, Swedish Agency for Cooperation with Developing Countries, Anders Wijkman, expressed his apprehension that if poverty continues like this in India "the social costs will be immense and eventually society will disintegrate."

A Study of the Jawahar Rozgar Yojana carried out by the Programme Evaluation Organisation of the Planning Commission (1992) states that the analysis of 43rd round of NSSO Survey (1987-88) revealed that a little over 90 percent of the rural poor below poverty line live in the ten major states of Andhra Pradesh, Bihar, Karnataka, Madhya Pradesh, Maharashtra, Orissa, Rajasthan, Tamil Nadu, Uttar Pradesh and West Bengal. It is not a coincidence that the Naxalites are active in varying degrees in these very states.

Land reforms are essential to any long term improvements in the agricultural sector. It encompasses (a) abolition of intermediaries, (b) tenancy reforms with security to actual cultivators, (c) redistribution of surplus ceiling land, (d) consolidation of holdings and (e) up-dating of land records. The intermediaries were done away with in the early

154

fifties with the abolition of Zamindari, which covered 40 percent of the land area in the country. There are tenancy laws in all the states except Nagaland, Meghalaya and Mizoram. These provide acquisition of ownership by tenants on payment of reasonable compensation, security of tenure and fixation of fair rent. The implementation of these laws in the states shows variations. West Bengal, Karnataka and Kerala have achieved a considerable measure of success. In West Bengal particularly, 14 lac sharecroppers have been recorded under the 'Operation Barga'. On the whole, however, as admitted by the Planning Commission, "tenancy reforms have not achieved the desired results as the incidence of informal, oral or concealed tenancies is very high."[13] Ceilings legislation were enacted in almost all the states, but here also "success has been limited due to poor enforcement."[14] Consolidation of holdings have made progress in some states, but in several states it is yet to make a beginning. Andhra Pradesh is one of the few defaulting states which has not enacted any legislation on the subject. The progress in updating of land records has been tardy.

The picture on the employment front is also dismal. An accelerated expansion of employment opportunities is necessary both for poverty alleviation and effective utilisation of human resources for economic and social development in the country. Unfortunately, however, there has been deceleration in the rate of growth of employment over the years. It was 2.82 percent during 1973-78, 2.2 percent during 1978-83 and is estimated to have been 1.55 percent during 1983-88. The situation is compounded by a faster increase in the labour force by about 2.5 percent. The backlog of unemployment, as a consequence, has been steadily rising. Some of the salient features of the unemployment situation in India are: its incidence is much higher in urban than in rural areas; unemployment rates for women are higher than those for men; under-employment among women is also in higher proportion; and the incidence of unemployment among the educated is much higher at about 12 per cent than the overall usual status unemployment of 3.77 percent.

The Scheduled Castes and Scheduled Tribes constitute the poorest of the poor sections. Their condition would best be described in the words of Planning Commission:

155

"...the incidence of poverty is still very high. Most of the Scheduled Caste and Scheduled Tribe families do not own land or other productive assets. They constitute bulk of agricultural landless workers, construction workers and workers in unorganised sector. They suffer from long periods of unemployment and under-employment. They are also handicapped due to non-enforcement of protective laws such as the Minimum Wages Act and Prevention of Land Alienation Acts. Inequality and exploitation of Scheduled Castes and Scheduled Tribes, particularly in the rural areas, whether in the form of bonded labour or in other forms, both latent and manifest, still continue. Poverty, ignorance, lack of options in employment opportunities and non-existence of organisations which can fight for their rights, facilitate the continuance of age old exploitation. Scheduled Caste and Scheduled Tribe families have often not been able to derive the full benefit of development programmes. Wrong identification of beneficiaries,poor selection of projects, unrealistic and simplistic assumptions in regard to their viability, administrative costs, and leakages have been other problems which have been further compounded by a largely unresponsive administrative structure.

The dwindling resource base of the tribal people in the shape of loss of land, restriction on access to forest produce, and lack of opportunities for reasonable wage employment and usurious money lending have caused hardships to tribal people. Consequently, developmental inputs for the benefit of these people have had little impact. Significantly, development processes have interfered in many cases with traditional tribal institutional structure and ethos and have produced negative results. These were contributory factors for dissatisfaction amongst tribal people and simmering unrest in some tribal areas."[15]

The dissatisfaction of the tribals arising out of their exploitation and oppression has led to their taking up arms in several areas. In fact, over the years, tribal insurgency has become the predominant strand of the Naxalite movement. It was there even in the earlier years of the movement in the sixties when there was unrest in Naxalbari, Gopiballavpur, Srikakulam and Lakhimpur-Kheri. The Government of India undertook development of the tribal areas with a view to integrate the tribal population into the mainstream. However, ironically, "the process of development, conceived as industrialisation, commercialisation and modernisation of the economy, has simultaneously led to the marginalisation and increasing deprivation of tribal communities—communities which are losing their traditional means of livelihood but are as yet unable to adjust to the pressures of a modern, competitive society."[16] Forest and forest produce have traditionally been the major source of livelihood for tribal communities. But the over-exploitation of forest resources in the wake of commercialisation and industrialisation has led to gradual erosion of the forest cover. This process was already there during the British period—it got accelerated during the post-independence industrialisation. By eighties, the forest cover was declining at the rate of over 56,000 sq. kms per annum. The depletion of forest resources subjected the tribal communities to great stress. In Bihar, the tribals have access to less than one third of the remaining forest resources, the rest being commercially exploited. In Orissa, the tribals have to travel about 7 kms a day now to collect forest products as against 1.7 Kms in the past. Another major source of deprivation for the tribals has been their displacement as a consequence of development projects. It is estimated that between 1951-1990, about 18.5 million persons were displaced by dams (14 million), mines (2.1 million), industries (1.3 million) and other projects (1.1 million). Out of these only 4.6 million persons could be rehabilitated, leaving a backlog of 13.9 million displaced persons, some of them more than once.[17]

The economic reforms programme initiated in 1991 has been implemented by the Government of India in two phases. The first phase, which is almost over, was concerned with stabilisation and involved mainly restraining the growth of aggregate demand. The second phase of structural adjustment is now under way and involves wide-ranging reforms affecting the basic structure and the growth path of the economy. The UNDP study is of the view that the stabilisation measures induced industrial recession and have involved cuts in public expenditure on anti-poverty programmes." As such, there can be little doubt that the employment generation and poverty alleviation processes, operative in the eighties, have been reversed in the course of stabilisa-

157

tion." Regarding the level of underemployment and the incidence of poverty, the UNDP study has expressed the view that these have "very probably increased since 1991 although this cannot be empirically confirmed."

Thus we come to a situation where we have a mass of humanity—the largest in the world—still living below the poverty line more than four decades after independence, where land reforms which are basic to any improvement in the agricultural sector have been implemented in a very half-hearted manner, where the backlog of unemployment continues to rise, where the tribals' rhythm of life has been seriously disturbed by an unimaginative development process, and where the poverty alleviation processes have lately been reversed. It would be no exaggeration to say that these factors are today present in a more acute and aggravated form than they were in the late sixties when the first spark appeared at Naxalbari.

The social tensions have, tragically, also got exacerbated. Earlier, it was a caste or a community holding the lower denomination in serfdom. Today, it is one community against another, one caste against another and even one sub-caste against another, thanks to the arbiters of our destiny who are in a rat race to appear as greater champions .of the *dalits* and backwards—more to get their votes than out of any sympathy for them. Disintegration rather than integration is the trend. The disastrous consequences of these myopic policies are there for anyone to see. The social fabric is in tatters and we have the macabre spectable of caste groups at each others' throats and people's heads being chopped off on locally contrived guillotines. Bihar had 300.3 lakhs of population below the poverty line in the year 1987-88, second only to that of UP. With such a large population of rural poor with a high level of social tension and with a political authority which exists more in name than in substance, it is no wonder that Bihar is heading for anarchical conditions. In the emerging grim scenario, Naxalite violence could register a sharp upward trend. There would no doubt be other points of friction as well. Uttar Pradesh unfortunately is following suit. Its rural population below the poverty line in 1987-88 was 373.1 lakhs. Here also the seeds of caste war are being sown. Pettifogging politicians forget that the foundations of any system of governance cannot be built on hatred and that by provoking one group of people against another, they are only going to create turmoil and internecine clashes in a society they have been entrusted to govern. UP and Bihar, between them, account for about one-third of the total number of rural poor living below the poverty line. The two states in the heartland of India present a frightening combination of economic poverty and escalating social tensions.

About the establishment, the less said the better. There is a general feeling of despair among the people over the way the executive, the legislature and the judiciary have been functioning. The executive's moral fibre is in shambles. The bureaucracy and the police, generally speaking, have no sense of dedication or commitment to the people. The legislatures are infiltrated with criminals. Not one political party has a clean image. Persons with shady background have managed to reach the level of Chief Minister in some states. One can only hope and pray that a Noriega does not preside over the destiny of this country from the South Block one day. The criminal justice system is crumbling. The Supreme Court, while granting stay on the *ex parte* order of Allahabad High Court in a case, deplored the "stinking mess in the administration of justice." There is an acute sense of disillusionment over prolonged delays, tortuous procedures and, at the end of it all, very poor convictions with the criminals and mafia dons having the last laugh.

The laws, rules and regulations are interpreted at the cutting edge level in a manner which suits the vested interests holding influential positions. This leads to avoidable conflict between the people and the establishment. The situation was beautifully summed up by the Commissioner for Scheduled Castes and Scheduled Tribes in his Twenty-ninth Report for the period 1987-89 in the following words:

"In this way the situation of forest is the same everywhere. There are a number of areas where there is direct confrontation between the government and the people such as Adilabad, Khammam and Srikakulam in Andhra Pradesh, South Bastar in Madhya Pradesh, Gadchiroli, Chandrapur and Nasik in Maharashtra and Singhbhum in Bihar. In many areas the forests are now out of effective control of the forest department. The situation everywhere has been deteriorating only because no attention has been paid to the

159

justifiable demands of the people; there have been attempts to superimpose laws unilaterally and the behaviour of the departmental officials has been authoritarian and oppressive. In the end either the people have risen in revolt on their own or the extremist forces took up their cudgels. It is regretted that no attention has been paid to the basic question of resolving this confrontation."

Elsewhere, the Commissioner deplored that the authorities who have been bestowed enormous powers for the protection and welfare of the tribal people have not been able to save them from the exploitation and oppression of government servants and that "this historic task has been accomplished only by the Naxalites in some areas."

The scenario is thus one of encircling gloom. There is economic poverty, exploitation and inequality. There is social oppression and injustice leading to fratricidal conflicts between castes and communities. Politically the system is stinking with corruption. It would however be naive so say that this combination would necessarily lead to a resurgence of the Naxalite movement in the country. Cause and effect are inextricably linked up, but what would be the precise effect of a certain set of factors in a given situation, is not easy to prognosticate. The environmental factors constitute an imponderable complex and these may catalyse or impede a particular process. There have already been certain regressive developments which are diverting people's energies negatively. These include the growth of religious fundamentalism, regional pulls, linguistic fanaticism and separatist movements. The Naxalite ideology seeks to cut across the barriers of caste and region and unite people on broader economic issues. So when the smaller, narrower forces get primacy, it is but natural that the macro issues would take the back-seat. And this is precisely what is happening in the country. Issues like building a temple or a mosque, giving recognition to a language or carving out a new state arouse fierce passions and generate more heat than alleviating poverty, removing unemployment or uplifting the poorest of the poor.

There are several theories on why people take up arms. Some describe insurgency as "deviant social behaviour", some attribute it to the break-up of traditional societies and the process of modernisation. The theory which has gained widest currency and has been accepted by Marxists and liberals alike is the "grievance-frustration" concept. As stated by Walter Laqueur, "men and women will not rebel, risking their lives and property, without good reason—the occupation of their country by foreign armies, economic crisis, a tyrannical political regime, great poverty, or great social discrepancy between rich and poor."[18] But this leads us to another question: how much of grievance or how much of frustration a society is prepared to accept or, in other words, what is its tolerance level? When is the breaking point reached? This again would differ from community to community and may even vary for the same community at different periods of time. Besides, grievance *per se* is not so relevant; what really matters is the perception of that grievance. The various theories throw light on a couple of insurgencies, but there is no theory which could explain the types and types of insurgencies the world has witnessed. Any generalisation on the subject is not possible. In our own country, we have seen people taking up arms against the government in different areas for altogether different reasons. What is significant is that the same reasons existing in other regions did not produce a similar violent outburst. Orissa is a peculiar case of a state having the maximum incidence of poverty, but the society there has a very high tolerance level and there has been nothing like a rebellion except some stirrings in the districts bordering Andhra Pradesh and West Bengal, where also it was a spill-over of Naxalite activities in those adjoining states. On the other hand, unemployment among the youth was one of the factors which contributed to terrorism in an otherwise affluent Punjab. The Nagas rebelled *inter alia* for ethnic reasons, but there are other tribes in bordering regions which have been living peacefully. According to De Tocqueville, people revolt not merely because they are poor and oppressed but mainly because "they are aware of a gulf between their expectations and their present conditions and of a possibility of crossing it by a single bound." To this we may add that a comparison of their state with the affluence of the rich who are getting richer would make them more impatient and highly vulnerable to any ideology which appeals to violence. These comparisons are today possible, thanks to the phenomenal improvements in the electronic and print media. Exploitation which could earlier continue unnoticed and unchallenged in a cobwebbed, shadowed corner of the country today gets known, and its knowledge is broadcast not only within but outside the country in no time. There are other factors also whose juxtaposition might accelerate the precipitation of crisis—a political turmoil, a severe economic crisis, or the emergence of a new leader. None of these factors could be ruled out in a country, India being no exception.

The factors which gave rise to Naxalism in the country are, in any case, very much present today also—and in an acute and aggravated form. The erosion of faith in the political processes, grinding poverty of a large mass of humanity, economic disparities and their realisation, mounting unemployment, tribal unrest, aggravating social tensions, and the failure of the administration to fulfil the rising expectations of the people are all bound to take their toll and lead to a highly surcharged and explosive situation. As things are, however, it is unlikely that there would be a countrywide revolution leading to overthrow of the system in the foreseeable future. The political formations and other representative bodies are embroiled in narrow regional, linguistic, caste-oriented, fundamentalist or sub-national issues and the conflicts arising therefrom. Besides, the Indian society, as a whole, has a very high tolerance level. This is its source of strength as also its weakness—strength because it allows free play to diverse schools of thought which ultimately go to enrich the Indian cultural mosaic and weakness because it allows muck to accumulate and the periodic cleaning up which has been the good fortune of Western societies does not take place. The grievance-frustration explosive would also require detonation, and that would be provided by a political or economic crisis only. Till then, the wretched of the earth—the exploited, the oppressed, the deprived and the alienated—with "furies and sorrows" in their hearts, as Francisco de Quevedo said, would continue their struggle against the system. The struggle areas may even witness a gradual enlargement. The embers would simmer and the fire would burn, now here and now there—in an agrarian area, an urban pocket or a tribal region, wherever popular discontentment against the system reaches a flash-point.

162

APPENDICES

APPENDIX A

PEOPLE'S DAILY
(July 5, 1967 Editorial)

Spring Thunder Breaks Over India

A peal of spring thunder has crashed over the land of India. Revolutionary peasants in the Darjeeling area have risen in rebellion. Under the leadership of a revolutionary group of the Indian Communist Party, a red area of rural revolutionary armed struggle had been established in India. This is a development of tremendous significance for the Indian people's revolutionary struggle.

In the past few months, the peasant masses in the Darjeeling area led by the revolutionary group of the Indian Communist Party have thrown off the shackles of modern revisionism and smashed the *trammels* that bound them. They have seized grain, land and weapons from the landlords and plantation owners, punished the local tyrants and wicked gentry, and ambushed the reactionary troops and police that went to suppress them, thus demonstrating the powerful might of the peasants' revolutionary armed struggle. All imperialists, revisionists, corrupt officials, local tyrants and wicked gentry, and reactionary army and police are nothing in the eyes of the revolutionary peasants who are determined to strike them down to the dust. *The revolutionary group of the Indian Communist Party have done the absolutely correct thing and they have done it well.* The Chinese people joyfully applaud this revolutionary storm of the Indian peasants in the Darjeeling area as do all Marxist-Leninists and revolutionary people of the whole world.

It is an inevitability that the Indian peasants will rebel and the

Indian people will make revolution because the reactionary Congress rule has left them with no alternative. India under Congress rule is only nominally independent; in fact it is nothing more than a semi-colonial, semi-feudal country. The Congress administration represents the interests of the Indian feudal princes, big landlords and bureaucrat-compradore capitalists. Internally, it oppresses the Indian people without any mercy and sucks their blood, while internationally it serves its new boss, US imperialism, and its number one accomplice, the Soviet revisionist ruling clique, in addition to its old suzerian British imperialism, thus selling out the national interests of India in a big way. So imperialism, Soviet revisionism, feudalism and bureaucrat-compradore capitalism weigh like big mountains on the backs of the Indian people, first of all on the toiling masses of workers and peasants.

The Congress administration has intensified its suppression and exploitation of the Indian people and pursued a policy of national betrayal during the past few years. Famine has stalked the land. The fields are strewn with the bodies of those who have died of hunger and starvation. The Indian people, above all the Indian peasants, have found life impossible for them. The revolutionary peasants in the Darjeeling area have now risen in rebellion, in violent revolution. This is the prelude to a violent revolution by the hundreds of millions of people throughout India. The Indian people will certainly cast away these big mountains off their backs and win complete emancipation. This is the general trend of Indian history which no force on earth can check or hinder.

What road is to be followed by the Indian revolution? This is a fundamental question affecting the success of the Indian revolution and the destiny of the 500 million Indian people. The Indian revolution must take the road of relying on the peasants, establishing base area in the countryside, persisting in protracted armed struggle and using the countryside to encircle and finally capture the cities. This is Mao Tse-tung's road, the road that has led the Chinese revolution to victory, and the only road to victory for the revolution of all oppressed nations and people.

Our great leader Chairman Mao Tse-tung pointed out as long as 40 years ago: "In China's central, southern and northern provinces, several hundred million peasants will rise like a mighty storm, like a hurricane, a force so swift and violent that no power, however great, will be able to hold it back. They will smash all the trammels that bind them and rush forward along the road to liberation. They will sweep all the imperialists, warlords, corrupt officials, local tyrants and evil gentry into their graves."

Chairman Mao has explicitly pointed out long ago that the peasant question occupies an extremely important place in the people's revolution. The peasants constitute the main force in the national democratic revolution against imperialism and its lackeys; they are the most reliable and numerous allies of the proletariat. India is a vast semi-colonial and semi-feudal country with a population of 500 million. The absolute majority of which is the peasantry. Once aroused, these several hundred million Indian peasants will become the invincible force of the Indian revolution. By integrating itself with the peasants, the Indian proletariat will be able to bring about earth-shaking changes in the vast countryside of India and defeat any powerful enemy in a soul-stirring people's war.

Our great leader Chairman Mao teaches us: "The seizure of power by armed force, the settlement of the issue by war, is the central task and the highest form of revolution. This Marxist-Leninist principle of revolution holds good universally, for China and for all other country."

The specific feature of the Indian revolution, like that of the Chinese revolution, is armed revolution fighting against armed counter-revolution. Armed struggle is the only correct road for the Indian revolution; there is no other road whatsoever. Such trash as "Gandhism", "parliamentary road" and the like are opium used by the Indian ruling classes to paralyse the Indian people. Only by relying on violent revolution and taking the road of armed struggle can India be saved and the Indian people achieve complete liberation. Specifically, this is to arouse the peasant masses boldly, build up and expand the revolutionary armed forces, deal blows at the armed suppression of the imperialists and reactionaries, who are temporarily stronger than the revolutionary forces, by using the flexible strategy and tactics of people's war personally worked out by Chairman Mao, and to persist in protracted armed struggle and seizing victory of the revolution step by step.

In the light of the characteristics of the Chinese revolution, our great leader Chairman Mao has pointed out the importance of establishing revolutionary rural base areas. Chairman Mao teaches us that in order to persist in protracted armed struggle and defeat imperialism and its lackeys, "it is imperative for the revolutionary ranks to turn the backward villages into advanced, consolidated base areas, into great military, political, economic and cultural bastions of the revolution from which to fight their vicious enemies who are using the cities for attacks on the rural districts, and in this way gradually to achieve the complete victory of the revolution through protracted fighting."

India is a country with vast territory; its countryside where the reactionary rule is weak, provides the broad areas in which the revolutionaries can manoeuvre freely. So long as the Indian proletarian revolutionaries adhere to the revolutionary line of Marxism-Leninism, Mao Tse-tung's thought and rely on the great ally, the peasants, it is entirely possible for them to establish one advanced revolutionary rural base area after another in the backward rural areas and build a people's army of a new type. Whatever difficulties and twists and turn the Indian revolutionaries may experience in the course of building such revolutionary base areas, they will eventually develop such areas from isolated points into a vast expanse, from small areas into extensive ones, an expansion in a series of waves. Thus, a situation in which the encirclement of the cities from the countryside will gradually be brought about in the Indian revolution to pave the way for the final seizure of towns and cities and winning nationwide victory.

The Indian reactionaries are panic-stricken by the development of the rural armed struggle in Darjeeling. They have sensed imminent disaster and they wail in alarm that the peasants' revolts in Darjeeling will "become a national disaster."

Imperialism and the Indian reactionaries are trying in a thousand and one ways to suppress this armed struggle of the Darjeeling peasants and nip it in the bud. The Dange renegede clique and the revisionist chieftains of the Indian Communist Party are vigorously slandering and attacking the revolutionaries in the Indian Communist Party and the revolutionary peasants in Darjeeling for their great exploits. The so-called "non-Congress government" in West Bengal openly sides with the reactionary Indian government in its bloody suppression of the revolutionary peasants in Darjeeling. This gives added proof that

168

these renegades and revisionists are running dogs of US imperialism and Soviet revisionism and lackeys of the big Indian land-lords and bourgeoisie. What they call the "non-Congress government" is only a tool of these landlords and bourgeoisie.

But no matter how well the imperialists, Indian reactionaries and the modern revisionists may cooperate in their sabotage and suppression, the torch of armed struggle lighted by the revolutionaries of the Indian Communist Party and the revolutionary peasants in Darjeeling will not be put out. "A single spark can start a prairie fire." The spark in Darjeeling will start a prairie fire and will certainly keep the vast expanses of India ablaze. That a great storm of revolutionary armed struggle will eventually sweep across the length and breath of India is certain. Although the course of the Indian revolutionary struggle will be long and tortuous, the Indian revolution, guided by great Marxism-Leninism, Mao Tse-tung's thought, will surely triumph.

APPENDIX B

Biographical Sketches on Some of the Leaders
Connected With the Naxalbari Peasant Uprising
and the Communist Party of India (Marxist-Leninist)

It is always imperative to collect exhaustive biographical information on the leading figures connected with a political movement of any kind in order to understand the social background of such a movement. Since the Naxalbari Peasant Uprising of 1967 and the subsequent Maoist movement in West Bengal, which was a byproduct of that uprising, created a great stir throughout the country during the last five years, it is all the more important to have accurate information on the social background of those who led the movement. Unfortunately however, because of the secrecy that has all the time pervaded the CPI (M-L) affairs since its formation, it has been rather difficult for the author to obtain adequate data on the social composition of the party's leadership. Nevertheless, great caution has been taken while collating information from diverse sources like the daily newspapers, journals and interviews with party activists. Some names, however, have been reluctantly left out only because no data were available.

Bose, Sourin

Born in 1925, at Alipurduar in the Jalpaiguri District; a graduate. Joined the CPI at a young age. Arrested during the Sino-Indian border war in 1962 for alleged anti-state activities; after release joined the CPI(M) in 1964. A member of the Darjeeling District Committee of the Party. Expelled from the Party along with Charu Mazumdar in 1967 for organising the Naxalbari Peasant Uprising. A founder-member of the Communist Party of India (Marxist-Leninist). Included in the

Party's Central Committee at its Foundation Congress held in 1970 and had discussion with some senior Chinese leaders at Peking over the tactics to be followed by the CPI (ML). On his return, developed ideological differences with Charu Mazumdar and joined Asim Chatterjee's faction.

Chatterjee, Asim

Born in 1944, son of a rich and influential Congressman of Birbhum, West Bengal. Known in the party circle as "Kaka" and "Khokan". Graduated from Presidency College, Calcutta. A leading figure in the Presidency College Students' Union controlled by the BPSF(L), the students' wing of the CPI(M). Expelled from the BPSF(L) for organising students' movements at the Presidency College and Calcutta University in support of the Naxalbari peasants. Formed a Marxist students' organisation—the Presidency College Students' Consolidation. In 1969 on Charu Mazumdar's call to work among the peasants in the countryside, Chatterjee along with his close associates, left for Debra-Gopiballavpur in Midnapur to organise agrarian movements. After the failure of the peasant movement in that area he developed differences over ideological-tactical questions especially over the Bangla Desh issue with his mentor, Charu Mazumdar and built up his own organisation, the Bengal-Bihar-Orissa Border Regional Committee. Formed an alliance with Satyanarain Sinha, Secretary, Bihar State Unit of the CPI(ML). Elected member of the party's Central Committee in 1970. Tried to organise "Red bases" in the countryside of Birbhum but failed. A "Proclaimed Offender" with an award of Rs. 5000 on his head, Chatterjee was arrested at Deoghar in November 1971.

Datta, Saroj

Born in 1913 at Jessore, East Bengal (now Bangla Desh); received education upto the Post Graduate standard. Took up the career of a journalist. Joined the *Amrita Bazar Patrika* as a sub-editor and rose to the position of Editor-in-Chief at the night shift of the daily's office. Lost his job in 1949 for participating in violent and subversive activities which the CPI had launched during the "left sectarian" period under the leadership of B.T. Ranadive. Known in the party circle for his extremist views; was one of the editors of the *Swadhinata*. Arrested in 1962 for anti-state activities; joined the CPI(M) after the split in the CPI in 1964; elected a member of the Calcutta District Committee of the party and appointed one of the members of the editorial board of the *Deshahitaishi*, weekly Bengali organ of the CPI(M) West Bengal state unit. Expelled from the party in 1967 for supporting the Naxalbari Peasant Uprising. Was one of the founder members of the Communist Party of India (Marxist-Leninist) and elected to the Central Committee of the Party. Appointed Editor-in-Chief of the *Deshabrati*, the weekly Bengali organ of the CPI(ML)'s West Bengal Unit after the dismissal of Sushital Roy Chaudhury (who had developed serious ideological differences with the Party Chief, Charu Mazumdar) from that post. Had a very powerful and facile pen and used to write under the pen-name "Sasanka".

Ghosh, Suniti

A former lecturer in English in the Vidyasagar College (Evening section), Calcutta, Ghosh was known to have always taken extreme positions in his political views. Became politically active after the Naxalbari Peasant Uprising of 1967 and joined the CPI (ML) in 1969. Was a close associated of Charu Mazumdar and elected to the Central Committee of the party. Took over charge of the CPI (ML) English organ, *Liberation* in 1971 as its Editor-in-Chief after the expulsion of Sushital Roy Chaudhury from the party. Wrote under the pen-name "Soumya".

Mazumdar, Charu

Son of Bireswar Mazumdar; born in a zamindar family of Siliguri, Darjeeling in 1918. Matriculated from the Siliguri Boys' School in 1936. Jointed the Edward College at Pabna (now in Bangladesh). In 1938 joined the then outlawed CPI and started working in the party's peasant front in the Jalpaiguri District. Organised the Tebhaga movement in the 1940's mainly in the three police stations of the Jalpaiguri District: Boda, Pachagarh, and Debiganj. After the failure of the movement, devoted himself to organising the workers of the then Bengal Dooars Railway at Domohani. Censured by the Jalpaiguri District Committee of the CPI for plunging the peasants of Boradighi Jote in the Dooar in a premature and militant movement which resulted in the firs police firing in the region leading to the death of 12 men and women.

During the period of Zhdanovist adventurism followed by the CPI under the Ranadive leadership in the late 1940's, Mazumdar organised the tea-garden workers of the Darjeeling District. Arrested in 1949. After release in 1952, resumed trade union activities. In early 1960's raised the banner of Maoist revolt against the "revisionist" leadership of the CPI. Arrested in 1960 for anti-state activities during the India-China border war. Released in 1963, contested a bye-election as the CPI candidate to the West Bengal Assembly from Siliguri and was defeated. After the split in the CPI in 1964 joined the CPI(M). In 1965 issued a circular in the name of the CPI(M); condemned and suspended temporarily by the party. In 1967 on the decision of the CPI(M) to join the United Front Government, wrote a series of eight letters to party members urging them to launch an immediate armed struggle on the Maoist line. Soon after installation of the UF Government he master-minded a peasant uprising in the Naxalbari area of Darjeeling district in the spring of 1967. Expelled from the CPI(M) for this towards the end of 1967. Formed the All-India Coordination Committee of the Communist Revolutionaries (AICCCR) in 1986. On May 1, 1969 the CPI(ML) was formed with Mazumdar as its first General Secretary. The party started disintegrating from the middle of 1971 when different leaders challenged Mazumdar's leadership and his tactical lines on "annihilation of class enemies" and urban guerrilla action. A "Proclaimed Offender" in 1971 with an award of Rs. 10,000 on his head, Mazumdar was arrested in Calcutta on July 16, 1972. Died of a heart attack on July 28, 1972 in the police custody at Lal Bazar, Calcutta.

Rana, Santosh

Born in a Scheduled Cast family in 1944 at Gopiballavpur in Midnapur, West Bengal; an M.Sc. from the University of Calcutta. Inducted into the Maoist movement in West Bengal immediately after the Naxalbari Peasant Uprising of 1967. Active in the PSCC, a Maoist students' organisation throughout 1968-1969. Organised peasant guerrilla warfare at Debra-Gopiballavpur, Midnapur District in 1967-1970. Elected to the CPI(ML) Central Committee in 1970. Developed tactical and ideological differences with Charu Mazumdar and joined Asim Chatterjee's Bengal-Bihar-Orissa Border Regional Committee. Married

Jayashri Rana, who had actively led the tribal peasants at Debra-Gopiballavpur. Arrested in early 1972.

Raychaudhury, Sushital

Born in 1917 at Hooghly in West Bengal; graduated from Calcutta University. Joined the Indian Communist movement at a very early age. Elected secretary of the Hooghly District Committee of the CPI in 1943. Wrote extensively in the party weekly *Swadhinata* and other papers like *Matamat* (Views), *Sambad* (News) on the *Tebhaga* movement in Bengal in the early 1940's. Transferred to the Calcutta District Committee of the party after independence and joined the editorial board of the *Swadhinata*. Gravitated to the Left Communist faction during the inner-party squabbles following the India-China border war of 1962. Joined the CPI(M) in 1964 and was elected to the editorial Board of *Deshahitaishi*, the Bengali weekly organ of the CPI(M) West Bengal State Unit. Known for his extremist views. In 1965 wrote a series of articles in *Chinta* (Thought), challenging the party programme as "revisionist". Formed an extremist organisation in the CPI(M), the Marx-Engels Institute to wage inner-party ideological struggle. Actively supported the Naxalbari Peasant uprising of 1967 and was expelled from the CPI(M). Became a founder-member of the CPI(ML) and elected to the party's Central Committee in 1970. Appointed Editor-in-Chief of *Deshabrati* and *Liberation*, the CPI(ML) Bengali and English organs. Subsequently, developed ideological differences with Charu Mazumdar and was expelled from the party. Died of a heart attack in early 1971.

Santhal, Jangal

A tribal of the middle peasant origin in the Naxalbari area, Santhal in known as a professional tribal revolutionary leader. As a member of the Siliguri Local Committee of the CPI(M), Santhal had been active in the peasant front. Elected President of the Siliguri Subdivisional Kisan Sabha. Contested for a seat in the Assembly as a CPI candidate in 1962 and in 1967 as a CPI(M) candidate; was defeated on both the occasions. Acted as the "field-commander" of the Kisan Samiti's operations against landlords in the Naxalbari area in 1967. Elected a Central Committee member of the CPI(ML) in 1970. Arrested in 1971.

Kanu Sanyal

Born in 1932 at Jalpaiguri, came in contact with Subhas Chandra Bose and learnt from him his early lessons in politics. Received early education at the Kurseong English School; joined the Jalpaiguri Ananda Chandra College at the Intermediate class, and became a very active leader of the BPSF, the students' wing of the CPI. Expelled from the college for organising a violent demonstration against Dr. B.C. Roy, the then Chief Minister of West Bengal, who was visiting the Jalpaiguri town. Joined the Darjeeling District Committee of the CPI and devoted himself as a full-time party worker among the Adivasis, poor peasants and agricultural labourers. Joined the CPI(M) in 1964 and became a close associate and right-hand man of Charu Mazumdar. Revolted against the CPI(M) leadership when the party became a partner at the UF Government in West Bengal and led the Naxalbari Peasant Uprising in the spring of 1967. Expelled from the party. Announced the formation of the CPI(ML) at a May Day rally in Calcutta in 1969. Elected Central Committee member of the party and held a position next to his mentor, Charu Mazumdar. A "Proclaimed Offender" with an award of Rs. 10,000 on his head, Sanyal was arrested at his Naxalbari hideout in early 1971.

Sen, Asit

Born at Rangpur in East Bengal (now in Bangladesh) in the early 1920's; a Science graduate from Calcutta University. Was active in the BPSF, the student's wing of the CPI in the late 1930's; elected Secretary of the Local Committee of the CPI at Rangpur, his hometown. Joined the *Swadhinata Unit* of the party in 1950. Transferred to the Park Circus Local Committee and put in charge of the Education Branch of the Committee. Joined the CPI(M) after the split in 1964. Supported the Maoist faction in the CPI(M) after the Naxalbari Peasant Uprising in 1967. Expelled from the party in late 1967. Presided over the May Day rally held in Calcutta in 1969 in which the formation of the Communist Party of India (Marxist-Leninist) was announced. Subsequently, developed ideological differences with Charu Mazumdar, resigned

175

from the CPI(ML) in early 1970 and formed a Maoist organisation, "The Preparatory Committee of the Revolutionary People's Struggle." Edited *Dakshin Desh* (Southern Country) and *Liberation War*, two Maoist journals.

Sen, Mary (*née Tyler*)

Born in London in 1943. Daughter of Earnest Tyler, a port superintendent in North London. Became a school teacher in Willsden High School after graduating from King's College, London. Connected with the Marxist circles in London. Met Amalendu Sen, a committed Marxist from India during one of her trips to West Germany. Came to India in late 1969 by an overland route and because of her association with Amalendu Sen, joined the Naxalite movement, then at its height. They were married in April 1970. Arrested along with 51 others on May 28, 1970 from the dense forests of Jamshedpur, Bihar, immediately after their abortive attack on a nearby police post for seizing arms. Very recently the Government of India has withdrawn all cases against her and she had been sent back to United Kingdom. Speaks English, German, Italian, Spanish, Latin, Hindi and Bengali.

Singh, Satyanarain

Born in Bihar in 1932. Singh started his political career as a Congress volunteer; participated in the Quit India movement as a Congress Socialist whose idol was then Jayaprakash Narayan; became a Communist while working as an aircraftsman in the Royal Indian Air Force; arrested for refusing to salute the Union Jack on 15 August 1947 and released at the intervention of Mr. Jawaharlal Nehru'. Joined the CPI(M) in 1964 and became a member of the party's Bihar Secretariat, became a Maoist in 1967 after the Naxalbari Peasant Uprising Organiser of the Naxalite movement in Mushahari, Bihar, Singh had been one of the closest associates of Charu Mazumdar at the initial stages. He was elected Secretary of the Bihar Committee of the CPI(ML) and a member of the party's Central Committee and politbureau. He staunchly defended Mazumdar's line when it came under attack from Nagi Reddy, Asit Sen and Parimal Dasgupta. In September 1970, he himself, however, questioned Mazumdar's line and in 1971 he along with several leaders of the CPI(ML) Central Committee met in Bihar to review the party line. They rejected the political line laid down by Charu Mazumdar, and removed him from the party. Subsequently, Singh was elected General Secretary of the party.

Source: Asish Kumar Roy, *The Spring Thunder And After*, Minerva Associates (Publications), Calcutta, 1975, pp.276-284.

APPENDIX C

OPEN LETTER

The following letter was reported to have been circulated by a number of CPI(M-L) leaders quite some time before Charu Mazumdar's arrest and death in jail.

Comrades,

We convey our revolutionary greetings to all. We feel that we are not competent to send you these suggestions, but owing to abnormal situation inside the Party now, we are compelled to take this course.

By this time, we hope, you all know that the great glorious and correct Chinese Communist Party had sent us most valuable fraternal suggestions in respect of our liberation struggle in India in the month of November, 1970.

We are citing certain excerpts of the valuable suggestions for our convenience. The suggestions are:

(1) The Chinese Party grew and developed by fighting alien trends—both left adventurism and right deviation.

(2) The Chinese Revolution became successful with three magic weapons, (a) the Party, (b) the People's Army and (c) the United Front.

(3) To call a Chairman of the Party as the Chairman of another party is wrong, and...it will wound the national sentiment of the working class of this country.

(4) Your idea of United Front is wrong. You have said that the United Front will come into being only after the formation of some base areas. This is a mechanical understanding. The United Front is a process. The United Front comes into being at every stage of struggle, and again it breaks down. This is not a permanent organisation. There

is no doubt that the worker-peasant unity is its main basis. But the main understanding behind the United Front is the unity between the exploiter and the exploited (those exploiters who are not the main target of the revolution). The characterisation of the bourgeoisie as a whole comprador is wrong.

(5) The formulation that the open trade union, open mass organisations and mass movements are out of date, and taking to secret assassination as the only way needs rethinking. Formerly we misunderstood your word 'annihilation'. We used to think that the idea is taken from our Chairman's war of annihilation. But from July 1970 issue of *Liberation* (the organ of CPI (ML)) we came to understand that this annihilation means secret assassination.

(6) You have applied Lin Piao's People's War Theory in a mechanical way. Lin's Guerrilla War theory is a military affair. During the anti-Japanese resistance war when we had an army of 10 lacs, some comrades in the army raised a slogan that positional warfare and mobile warfare are the way to mobilise the people. In reply to this wrong theory, Comrade Lin said that guerrilla war is the only way to mobilise the people. This military theory has no relation with political and organisational question.

(7) Regarding the formulation that if a revolutionary does not make his hand red with the blood of class enemies, then he is not a Communist: If this be the yardstick of a Communist then that Communist Party cannot remain a Communist Party.

(8) No stress has been given on agrarian revolution and the slogan for the seizure of state power is counterpoised to the land problem. There is no agrarian programme.

(9) Without mass struggle and mass organisation, the peasants' armed struggle cannot be sustained. The Communist Party of China supported Naxalbari struggle not merely as a struggle for the seizure of state power. The article *Spring Thunder* published in China in support of Naxalbari and later published in *Liberation* will clarify it.

(10) The authority and prestige of a leader cannot be created but grow and develop.

(11) The general orientation of (CPI(ML)) is correct but its policy is wrong.

We firmly accept these valuable suggestions and criticism from

179

the fraternal Party. We deeply feel that the Central Committee of our Party led by Comrade Charu Mazumdar should have accepted the above suggestions and criticism at once and made self-criticism and rectify the mistakes, suggested, in the interest of the agrarian revolution of our country.

But to our great disappointment, regret and disgust, we found that Comrade Charu Mazumdar and the Central Committee led by him, has refused to take lessons from the above valuable suggestions. In our opinion, if he had any reservations in respect of the suggestions from the fraternal Party, then he could have readily circulated the fraternal Party's suggestions to all the Party units for discussion. But he failed to take this course, as a result of which discussion and discord cropped up inside the Party. This is the bad old method and practice followed inside the Indian Communist movement.

We firmly believe that the Central Committee and the Central Party line have deviated from the path of the glorious Naxalbari Peasant Uprising. That is, the path shown in their Report on Peasant Movement in the main has completely departed from the path enunciated in the famous article *Spring Thunder* in respect of our armed agrarian revolution. We deeply feel that our policy suffered Left adventurist deviations as a result of which a wrong left adventurist method was adopted for which at present the Party in fact has split into groups and factions and Comrade Sushital Roy Choudhury was the victim of this method and for this the cause of the armed agrarian revolution of our country is hindered and jeopardised.

We firmly declare that we do not owe any allegiance to any group or faction. Our relation with the groups which believed in the Thoughts of Mao, both inside and outside the CPI(ML), is not antagonistic. We firmly believe that as General Secretary of the Party, Comrade Charu Mazumdar is mainly responsible for the left adventurist deviations and at the same time, we firmly believe that all the members of the former first Central Committee elected by the first Congress of the Party and all the members co-opted in the present Central Committee cannot also shirk their responsibilities, because they are also more of less directly or indirectly responsible for the Left adventurist deviations.

We, the undersigned, with utmost devotion and frankness accept our guilt and we emphatically declare that we will boldly accept the criticisms of our comrades in this connection, and we are also doing our self-criticisms with full honesty. We call upon all the members of the former and the present Central Committee to accept their guilt and make self-criticism in the interest of our armed agrarian revolution.

We earnestly request all the members of our Party and the sympathisers to be bold enough and come forward unhesitatingly to repudiate the Left adventurist deviationist line advocated by Comrade Charu Mazumdar and ask him to make honest self-criticism and to accept his guilt in respect of our armed agrarian revolution. We also appeal to our comrades and sympathisers to criticise the Central Committee members and ask them to accept their guilt and make self-criticism honestly. We must be very careful against revisionism, while fighting against Left deviations, which have become the main danger inside the Party for the present.

We appeal earnestly to all the members of our Party to prepare a review of the struggle in their respective areas; start discussions throughout the Party; and try to rectify the mistakes in the light of the Naxalbari path as laid down in the article *Spring Thunder*, and by accepting the suggestion from the great, glorious and correct Chinese Communist Party as the basis, without any reservations and create a new unity to carry forward the armed agrarian struggle.

> *Kanu Sanyal*
> *Chowdhary Tejeswara Rao*
> *Souren Bose*
> *D. Nagabhusanam Patnaik*
> *Kolla Venkaiah*
> *D. Bhuvan Mohan Patnaik*

Source: *Naxalbari And After, A Frontier Anthology.* Edited by Samar Sen, Debrabrata Panda and Ashish Lahiri, Kathashilpa, Calcutta, 1978, pp. 322-326.

APPENDIX D

Number and Percentage of Population Below Poverty Line by States, 1972-73 (Officially Released Estimates)

S.No.	State	Rural		Urban		Combined	
		No. Lakhs	%age	No. Lakhs	% age	No. Lakhs	%age
(0)	(1)	(2)	(3)	(4)	(5)	(6)	(7)
1.	Andhra Pradesh	207.1	57.7	38.5	43.8	245.6	54.9
2.	Assam	69.0	48.2	4.9	33.8	73.9	47.0
3.	Bihar	291.2	55.8	25.9	43.4	317.1	54.5
4.	Gujarat	86.9	43.9	26.6	34.0	113.5	41.1
5.	Haryana	18.4	21.5	5.6	29.9	24.0	23.1
6.	Himachal Pradesh	5.1	15.5	0.3	12.5	5.4	15.1
7.	Jammu & Kashmir	14.1	36.1	4.7	51.6	18.8	39.0
8.	Karnataka	119.0	52.3	34.3	45.8	153.3	50.5
9.	Kerala	106.4	57.8	19.2	52.7	125.6	56.9
10.	Madhya Pradesh	222.3	61.4	32.5	44.8	254.8	58.6
11.	Maharashtra	191.5	53.9	56.7	34.3	248.2	47.7
12.	Manipur	2.4	24.7	0.4	24.2	2.8	24.7
13.	Meghalaya	1.8	20.6	0.2	10.8	2.0	19.0
14.	Orissa	147.3	71.0	8.5	43.3	155.8	68.6
15.	Punjab	22.6	21.5	7.3	21.8	29.9	21.5
16.	Rajasthan	105.0	47.5	18.8	39.3	123.8	46.0
17.	Tamil Nadu	183.5	63.0	67.8	52.2	251.3	59.7
18.	Tripura	6.2	42.6	0.3	18.7	6.5	39.9
19.	Uttar Pradesh	413.1	53.0	66.4	51.6	479.5	52.8
20.	West Bengal	220.9	64.0	41.6	35.9	262.5	56.8
21.	Nagaland and All Union Territories	8.4	37.6	12.8	26.7	21.2	30.2
	All India	2442.2	54.1	473.3	41.2	2915.5	51.5

Notes: (1) The above estimates are derived by using the poverty lines of Rs. 41 and Rs. 47 per capita per month for rural and urban areas respectively at 1972-73 prices, corresponding to the poverty lines of Rs. 49.1 and Rs. 56.6 respectively at 1973-74 prices.

(2) The number of persons below poverty line relates to the population as on 1st Oct., 1972.

Source: *Report of The Expert Group on Estimation of Proportion and Number of Poor,* Perspective Planning Division, Planning Commission, Government of India, New Delhi, July, 1993, p. 16.

APPENDIX E

Number and Percentage of Population Below Poverty Line by States 1987-88 (Officially Released Estimates)

S.No.	State	Rural		Urban		Combined	
		No. Lakhs	%age	No. Lakhs	% age	No. Lakhs	%age
(0)	(1)	(2)	(3)	(4)	(5)	(6)	(7)
1.	Andhra Pradesh	153.1	33.8	42.6	26.1	195.7	31.7
2.	Assam	50.4	24.5	2.5	9.4	52.9	22.8
3.	Bihar	300.3	42.7	36.1	30.0	336.4	40.8
4.	Gujarat	56.2	21.2	17.1	12.9	73.3	18.4
5.	Haryana	13.5	11.7	4.7	11.7	18.2	11.6
6.	Himachal Pradesh	4.4	9.7	0.1	2.4	4.5	9.2
7.	Jammu & Kashmir	8.4	15.5	1.4	8.4	9.8	13.9
8.	Karnataka	102.8	35.9	33.7	24.2	136.5	32.1
9.	Kerala	37.4	16.4	11.6	19.3	49.0	17.0
10.	Madhya Pradesh	194.0	41.5	30.9	21.3	224.9	36.7
11.	Maharashtra	166.9	36.7	47.2	17.0	214.1	29.2
12.	Orissa	124.2	48.3	10.9	24.1	135.1	44.7
13.	Punjab	9.6	7.2	4.3	7.2	13.9	7.2
14.	Rajasthan	80.5	26.0	19.0	19.4	99.5	24.4
15.	Tamil Nadu	138.4	39.5	38.5	20.5	176.9	32.8
16.	Uttar Pradesh	373.1	37.2	75.2	27.2	448.3	35.1
17.	West Bengal	137.2	30.3	36.3	20.7	173.5	27.6
18.	Small States & UT's	9.3	11.8	4.9	4.7	14.2	7.7
	All India	1959.7	33.4	417.0	20.1	2376.7	29.9

Notes: (1) The above estimates are derived by using the poverty line of Rs. 131.8 per capita per month for rural areas and 152.1 per capita per month for urban areas at 1987-88 prices, corresponding to the poverty lines of Rs. 49.1 and Rs. 56.6 respectively for 1973-74.
(2) The number of persons below poverty line relates to the population as on 1st March, 1988.

Source: *Report of The Expert Group on Estimation of Proportion and Number of Poor,* Perspective Planning Division, Planning Commission, Government of India, New Delhi, July, 1993, p. 19.

REFERENCES

Chapter 1—Stirrings in Naxalbari
1. Kanu Sanyal, Report on the Peasant Movement in the Terai Region, *Liberation*, November 1968, p.39.
2. Biplab Dasgupta, *The Naxalite Movement*, p.18.
3. Sumanta Banerjee, *In the Wake of Naxalbari*, p.118.
4. Naxalbari: Evidence and Inference, *NOW*, July 7, 1967.
5. *On Left Deviation*, Resolution of the Central Committee, Communist Party of India(Marxist), Madurai, August 18 to 27, 1967 and other Information Documents.
6. Kanu Sanyal, Report on the Peasant Movement in the Terai Region, *Liberation*, November 1968, p.32.
7. The Naxalbari Story, *Link*, August 15, 1967, p.84.
8. *Liberation*, November 1968, pp. 28-53.
9. Samar Sen, *Naxalbari and After, A Frontier Anthology*, Foreword.
10. Pravat Jana, The Main Danger, *Naxalbari and After, A Frontier Anthology*, Volume II, p.143.
11. *Liberation*, November 1968, p.45.
12. *Naxalbari and After, A Frontier Anthology*, Volume II, pp. 345-346.

Chapter 2
2.1 A New Party is Born
1. *On Left Deviation*, Resolution of the Central Committee, Communist Party of India, Madurai, August 18 to 27, 1967, p.14.
2. Ibid. p.17.
3. Ibid. p.16.
4. *Letter to Andhra Comrades*, CPI(M) publication, pp. 31-32.
5. *Divergent Views Between Our Party and the CPC on Certain Fundamental Issues of Programme and Policy*, CPI(M) publication, p.20.
6. *Ideological Debate Summed up by Politbureau*, CPI(M) publication, pp. VIII-IX.
7. Charu Mazumdar, It is Time to Build up a Revolutionary Party, *Liberation*, November 1967, pp. 62-63.
8. Declaration of the Revolutionaries of the CPI(M), *Liberation*, December 1967, pp 5-6.

9. Charu Mazumdar, The Indian People's Democratic Revolution, *Liberation*, June 1968, p. 12.

10. *Liberation*, June 1968, p. 30.

11. *Liberation*, November 1968, pp. 22-27.

12. Resolution on Andhra State Co-ordination Committee, *Liberation*, March 1969, p.9.

13. It is Time to Form the Party, *Liberation*, March 1969, p. 5.

14. Ibid, p.6.

15. N. Sanmugathasan, Indian Revolution to Success, *Liberation*, November 1967, p.50.

16. *Liberation*, May 1969, p.25.

17. *Naxalbari and After, A Frontier Anthology*, Vol.II pp. 251-263.

18. Op. Cit., pp. 263-274.

19. Historic May Day Rally in Calcutta, *Liberation*, May 1969, p. 121.

20. *Liberation*, July 1969, pp. 21-22.

2.2 *Ideas That Ignited*

1. *Liberation*, September-December 1970, p.22.

2. *Liberation*, May-July 1970, p.23.

3. *Liberation*, December 1969, p.80.

4. *Liberation*, November 1969, p.10.

5. *Liberation*, February 1970, pp.21-22.

6. Biplab Dasgupta, Naxalite Armed Struggles and the Annihilation Campaign in Rural Areas, *Economic and Political Weekly*, Annual Number, 1973, pp. 173-187

7. *Liberation*, January 1970, p.2.

8. *Naxalbari and After, A Frontier Anthology*, Vol.II, pp. 275-291

9. Op. Cit., pp. 283-284

10. Op. Cit., pp. 285-291

11. Op. Cit., pp. 291-296.

Chapter 3
3.1 *Andhra Pradesh—Srikakulam*

1. Subba Rao, Revolt in Srikakulam, *The Times of India*, January 4, 1970.

2. Report on Peasants' Armed Struggle in Srikakulam, *Liberation*, May 1969, p.62.

3. Subba Rao, Revolt in Srikakulam, *The Times of India*, January 4, 1970.

4. Report on the Girijan Struggle, *Liberation*, December 1968, p.41.

5. Report on Peasants Armed Struggle in Srikakulam, *Liberation*, May 1969, pp 60-61.

6. The Revolutionary Girijans are Learning Warfare through Warfare, *Liberation*, February 1969, p. 16.

7. Report on Peasants Armed Struggle in Srikakulam, *Liberation*, May 1969, p.68.

8. Srikakulam—Will it be the Yenan of India? *Liberation*, March 1969, pp. 66-69.

9. V.M. Nair, Extent of Naxalite Revolt in Andhra Pradesh, *Statesman*, December 10, 1969.

10. *Naxalites Violence in Andhra Pradesh*, Published by the Director of Information, Public Relations and Tourism, Government of Andhra Pradesh, Hyderabad.

11. *Liberation*, June 1969, p.14.

12. *Liberation*, May 1969, pp.83-84.

13. C. Chandra Sekhara Rao, What To Do?, *Naxalbari And After, A Frontier Anthology*, Volume I, p.101.

14. To the Staunch Fighters of Andhra Pradesh, *Liberation*, July 1971-January 1972, pp.2-4

3.2 *West Bengal—Midnapur and Birbhum*

1. Revolutionary Armed Peasant Struggle in Debra, West Bengal, *Liberation*, December 1969, p.65.

2. Sankar Ghosh, New Naxalite Strategy, *The Times of India*, October 27, 1969.

3. Kalyan Chowdhury, Focus on Midnapur, *Frontier*, December 6, 1969, p.7.

4. *The Times of India*, December 7, 1969.

5. Biplab Dasgupta, Naxalite Armed Struggles and the Annihilation Campaign in Rural Areas, *Economic and Political Weekly*, Annual Number 1973, p.181.

3.3 *Bihar and Uttar Pradesh*

1. N K Singh, Naxalites in Bihar: Fight for Land, *Patriot*, October 11, 1969.

2. Satyanarain Singh, Mushahari and its Lessons, *Liberation*, October 1969, p.22.

3. Advance of Armed Peasants' Guerilla Struggle in North Bihar, *Liberation*, May 1969, pp. 80-81.

4. On the Struggle of the Adivasi People against Oppression and Exploitation, *Liberation*, July 1968, p.53.

5. N K Singh, Naxalite in Chotanagpur, *Frontier*, Febuary 13, 1971, pp. 8-10.

6. Mary Tyler, *My Years in an Indian Prison*, p.191.

7. Armed Peasant Struggle in the Palia area of Lakhimpur, *Liberation*, April 1969, p.53.

8. *Indian Express*, May 9, 1969.

9. Biplab Dasgupta, Naxalite Armed Struggles and the Annihilation Campaign in Rural Areas, *Economic and Political Weekly*, Annual Number 1973, p. 183.
10. Swift Advance of Peasant Guerilla Struggle in Uttar Pradesh, *Liberation*, May-July 1970, pp. 107-110.
11. Ibid, p.53.

Chapter 4—The Blaze
1. *Liberation*, September-December 1970, p.4.
2. *Liberation*, March 1970, pp. 87-88.
3. *Liberation*, March 1970, p.7.
4. *Liberation*, August 1970, pp. 5-6.
5. *Newsweek*, June 8, 1970, p.15.
6. Ranjit Gupta, The Revolution That Failed, *The Illustrated Weekly of India*, April 21, 1985.
7. *Liberation*, September-December, 1970.
8. *Liberation*, January-March 1971, pp. 6-9.

Chapter 5
5.1 Cracks in the Party
1. Steeplechase in Birbhum, *Statesman*, August 24 and 25, 1971.
2. Based on: (i) *Liberation*, September-December 1970, pp.16-30 (ii) *Liberation*, April-June 1971, pp.10-11 (iii) *Liberation* (S.N. Singh Group), Vol 5, Nos. 1-2, 1971 pp. 9-41.
3. *Naxalbari and After, A Frontier Anthology*, Vol II, pp. 312-326 and *India Today*, May 16-31, 1979, pp.70-71
4. *Liberation* (S. N. Singh Group), Vol 5, Nos. 1-2, 1971, p.13.
5. *The Times of India*, April 14, 1971.
6. Mira Sinha, China Keeps its Option Open, *The Times of India*, July 9, 1971.
7. Naxalites: New Responses, *Hindustan Times*, May 30, 1971.
8. *Anand Bazar Patrika*, April 18, 1971. *The Times of India*, April 23, 1971.
9. Naxalism, The New Opium, *Statesman*, February 20, 1972.
10. Biplab Dasgupta, Naxalite Armed Struggles and the Annihilation Campaign in Rural Areas, *Economic and Political Weekly*, Annual Number 1973, p.173.

5.2 Post-Mazumdar Period
1. Kalyan Mukherjee and Rajendra Singh Yadav, *Bhojpur, Naxalism In The Plains Of Bihar*, p. 35.
2. Sachchidanand Pandey, *Naxal Violence*, p. 140.
3. *Statesman*, April 11, 1977.

4. *Statesman*, April 24, 1978.
5. *Pioneer*, June 27, 1981.

Chapter 6
6.1 People's War Group—Andhra, Madhya Pradesh & Maharashtra

1. Causes of Spurt in Naxalite Violence, *Indian Express*, September 1,1987.
2. Why Naxalism flourishes in Telengana, *The Times of India*, January 5, 1990.
3. The six vices were: i) Womanising ii) Extravagance iii) Bureaucracy iv) Unholy alliances v) Legalism vi) Technical mistakes.
4. Chidanand Rajghatta, Madiga Malliah Inherits the Earth, *The Times of India*, December 9, 1990.
5. Terror in Telengana, *Indian Express*, August 13, 1989.
6. Naxalites: New Tactics, *Frontline*, September 5-18, 1987, p. 100.
7. Venu Menon, Fear is the Key, *The Illustrated Weekly of India*, January 24-30, 1988.
8. Chidanand Rajghatta, *The Times of India*, December 9, 1990.
9. *Indian Express*, April 5, 1990.
10. *The Illustrated Weekly of India*, September 3,1989
11. *The Times of India*, July 17, 1988.
12. *Report of The Commissioner for Scheduled Castes and Scheduled Tribes*, Twenty-ninth Report, 1987-89, p.171.

6.2 The 'New Left' in Bihar

1. Arvind N. Das, *The Republic of Bihar*, p.XIV
2. Ibid, p.107.
3. Amiya K. Samanta, *Left Extremist Movement in West Bengal*, p.216.
4. Bindeshwar Pathak, *Rural Violence in Bihar*, p.98.
5. Sumitra Jain, Rural Violence in Bihar, *Link*, July 1987.
6. Farzand Ahmed, Crime As Punishment, *India Today*, August 31, 1993.
7. *The Times of India*, October 26, 1988.
8. *The Times of India*, October 10, 1990.
9. *The Times of India*, December 26, 1992. *Hindustan Times*, December 26, 1992. *Pioneer*, December 30, 1992.

Chapter 7—Retrospect and Prospect

1. *The Times of India*, February 15, 1989.
2. *Hindustan Times*, November 26 and 27, 1993.
3. *The Illustrated Weekly of India*, August 15-21, 1992.
4. Biplab Dasgupta, *The Naxalite Movement*, p.236.

5. *Hindustan Times*, November 26, 1993.
6. Arvind N. Das, *The Republic of Bihar*, p.72.
7. *Economic and Political Weekly*, March 2, 1985, pp.343-344
8. *India: Employment, Poverty and Economic Policies*, A Report prepared under a Project sponsored by the UNDP under Technical Support Services 1(December 1993)
9. Montek S. Ahluwalia, India's Economic Performance, Policies and Prospects, *The Indian Economy* edited by Robert E B Lucas and Gustav F Papanek, p.358.
10. Jayati Ghosh and Krishna Bharadwaj, Poverty and Employment in India, *Rural Livelihoods* edited by Henry Bernstein, Ben Crow and Hazel Johnson, pp.140-141
11. Op. Cit., pp.143-144
12. China is also facing this problem. A recent Xinhua despath from Beijing noted that while disparities have always existed because of "geological, historical and cultural" reasons, Central and Western China contain no fewer than 295 of the national total of 328 counties which are poverty stricken.
13. *Eighth Five Year Plan*, Vol II, p.33.
14. Op Cit., pp. 33-34.
15. Op Cit., p.420.
16. W. Fernandes, S. Chaudhury, M. Rao and N. Mishra, Deforestation, Displacement and Impoverishment of Tribals: Are Tribal Sub-Plans the Solution?,(mimeo) *ILO-ARTEP*, 1993.
17. Ibid. Cited in India: Employment, Poverty and Economic Polices', *ILO-ARTEP, 1993*, p.70.
18. Walter Laqueur, *Guerilla, A Historical and Critical Study*, p.387.

SELECT BIBLIOGRAPHY

GENERAL READING

1. Banerjee, Sumanta. *In the Wake of Naxalbari, A History of the Naxalite Movement in India.* Subarnarekha, Calcutta, 1980.
2. Burton, Anthony. *Urban Terrorism,* Leo Cooper, London, 1975.
3. Das, Arvind N. *The Republic of Bihar,* Penguin, New Delhi 1992.
4. Dasgupta, Biplab. *The Naxalite Movement,* Allied Publishers, New Delhi, 1975.
5. Debray, Regis. *Revolution in the Revolution?* Pelican Books, 1968.
6. Debray, Regis. *Strategy for Revolution,* Jonathan Cape, 1970.
7. Djilas, Milovan. *The New Class,* Thomas and Hudson, London, 1957.
8. Donald, J. Hanle. *Terrorism—The Newest Face of Warfare,* Pergamon-Brassey's International Defense Publishers, Inc. USA, 1989.
9. Ghosh, Sankar. *The Naxalite Movement, A Maoist Experiment,* Firma K.L. Mukhopadhyay, Calcutta, 1975.
10. Giap, Vo Nguyen. *Peoples War, Peoples Army,* Bantam, 1968
11. Gott, Richard. *Rural Guerillas in Latin America,* The Pelican Latin American Library.
12. Guevara, Ernesto. *On Guerilla Warfare,* Cassell, 1962.
13. Guevara, Ernesto. *Bolivian Diary,* Jonathan Cape, 1968.
14. Guevara, Ernesto. *Reminiscences of the Cuban Revolutionary War,* Pelican Books, 1969.
15. Irani, C.R. *Bengal, The Communist Challenge,* Lalvani Publishing House, Bombay, 1968.
16. Johari, Dr. J C. *Naxalite Politics in India.* Research Publications (The Institute of Constitutional and Parliamentary Studies), Delhi, 1972.
17. Kitson, Frank. *Low Intensity Operations,* Faber and Faber, London, 1975.
18. Labrousse, Alain. *The Tupamaros,* Penguin Books Ltd. England, 1973.

19. Liqueur, Walter. *Guerilla, A Historical and Critical Study*, Western Press, Boulder and London, 1984.

20. Manoranjan Mohanty. *Revolutionary Violence, A Study of the Maoist Movement In India*, Sterling Publishers Pvt. Ltd, Delhi, 1977.

21. Mao, Tse-tung. *Selected Military Writings of Mao Tse-tung*, Foreign Language Press, Peking, 1968.

22. Marighela, Carlos. *Minimanual of Urban Guerillas*, The Pelican Latin American Library.

23. Moss, Robert. *Urban Guerillas*, Temple Smith.

24. Mukherjee, Kalyan and Yadav, Rajendra Singh. *Bhojpur, Naxalism in the Plains of Bihar*, Radha Krishna Prakashan, Delhi, 1980.

25. Myrdal, Gunnar. *Asian Drama, An Inquiry into the Poverty of Nations*, Pantheon, New York, 1968.

26. O'Neill, Bard E. *Insurgency & Terrorism*, Brassey's (US) Inc. 1990.

27. Pandey, Sachchidanand. *Naxal Violence, A Socio-Political Study*, Chanakya Publications, Delhi, 1985.

28. Pathak, Bindeshwar. *Rural Violence in Bihar*, Concept Publishing Company, New Delhi, 1993.

29. Ram, Mohan. *Indian Communism, Split Within a Split*, Vikas Publications, New Delhi, 1969.

30. Ram, Mohan. *Maoism in India*, Vikas Publications, Delhi, 1971.

31. Ray, Rabindra. *The Naxalites and their Ideology*, Oxford University Press, Delhi, 1988.

32. Roy, Asish Kumar. *The Spring Thunder and After, A Survey of the Maoist and Ultra-Leftist Movements in India, 1962-75*, Minerva Associates (Publications) Pvt. Ltd, Calcutta, 1975.

33. Samanta, Amiya. K. *Left Extremist Movement in West Bengal, An Experiment in Armed Agrarian Struggle*, Firma K L M Private Ltd, Calcutta, 1984.

34. Sengupta, Bhabani. *Communism in Indian Politics*, Columbia University Press, New York and London, 1972.

35. Sen, Samar; Panda, Debabrata and Lahiri, Ashish. *Naxalbari and After, A Frontier Anthology*, Vols I & II, Calcutta, 1978.

36. Sinclair, Andrew. *Guevara*, Fontana/Collins, London, 1970.

37. Sinha, V.B. *The Red Rebel In India, A Study of Communist Strategy & Tactics*, Associated Publishing House, New Delhi, 1968.

38. Strong, Simon. *Shining Path, The World's Deadliest Revolutionary Force*, Harper Collins, London.

39. Thompson, Robert. *Defeating Communist Insurgency*, Chatto and Windus, 1967.

40. Tripathy, Biswakesh. *Terrorism and Insurgency in India*, Pacific Press, Orissa, India, 1987.

PAMPHLETS/BOOKLETS

1. *Communist Party and Naxalites*, Pratap Mitra and Mohit Sen, Communist Party Publication, New Delhi, 1971.

2. *Economic and Political Weekly*, Annual Number 1973, A Sameeksha Trust Publication, Vol. VIII Nos 4-6.

3. *Ideological Resolution*, Communist Party of India (Marxist), Adopted by the Central Plenum, Burdwan, April 5-12, 1968.

4. *Letter to Andhra Comrades*, Communist Party of India (Marxist) Publication.

5. *On Left Deviation*, Resolution of the Central Committee, Communist Party of India (Marxist), Madurai, August 1967, and other Information Documents.

6. *Report of the Commissioner for Scheduled Castes and Scheduled Tribes*, Twenty-ninth Report 1987-89.

7. *Stand on Ideological Issues*, Communist Party of India (Marxist), 1969.

8. *Statement of Inspector-General of Police on the Naxalite/Extremist Activity in Andhra Pradesh (1968-1977)*, Hyderabad, 1977.

9. *The Historic Telengana Struggle, Some Useful Lessons from its Rich Experience*, C. Rajeswara Rao, Communist Party Publication, New Delhi, 1972.

10. *The Naxalite Movement in Bihar* by B N Sinha.

INDIAN ECONOMY

1. *Alternative Economic Survey 1993-94*, Public Interest Research Group, New Delhi, April 1994.

2. *Eighth Five Year Plan, 1992-97*, Vols I & II, Planning Commission, New Delhi.

3. *India: Employment, Poverty and Economic Policies*, United Nations Development Programme, ILO, ARTEP, New Delhi, December, 1993.

4. *India, Poverty, Employment and Social Services*, A World Bank Country Study.

5. *Jawahar Rozgar Yojna—A Quick Study*, 1991-92, Programme Evaluation Organisation, Planning Commission (GOI), New Delhi, 1992.

6. *Report of the Expert Group on Estimation of Proportion and Number of Poor*, Perspective Planning Division, Planning Commission, GOI, New Delhi, July 1993.

7. *Rural Livelihoods, Crises and Responses*, Henry Bernstein, Ben Crow, Hazel Johnson, Oxford University Press in association with The Open University, 1992.

8. *The Indian Economy: Recent Development and Future Prospects*, Edited by Robert E.B. Lucas & Gustav F. Papanek, Oxford University Press, 1988.

GLOSSARY

adivasi	original inhabitant, tribal
ammavasi	dark night
banihar	daily wage-earner
bargadar	share-cropper
basti	locality
begar	labour not paid for
benami	in somebody else's name
dalam	guerilla squad
gaon	village
gherao	a form of protest in which there is wrongful confinement
girijan	hill people, tribals
jotedar	landlord
khet	field
kisan	farmer
lathi	a wooden stick
latheith	a person wielding a lathi
mazdoor	labourer
Musahar	a scheduled caste
sahukar or *shahukar*	trader

Note: © Copyright Government of India, 1994. Based upon Survey of India map with the permission of the Surveyor General of India. The responsibility for the correctness of internal details rests with the publisher. The territorial waters of India extend into the sea to a distance of twelve nautical miles measured from the appropriate base line. The boundary of Meghalaya shown on this map is as interpreted from the North-Eastern Areas (Reorganisation) Act, 1971, but has yet to be verified. The external boundaries and coast lines of India agree with the Record/Master Copy certified by Survey of India.

INDEX

Abad group, 53
Achuthan, A., 64
Adibhatla Kailasam, 46
Adilabad district, 111, 114
Adivasi Kisan Mazdoor
    Sangathan, 117
Agressive peasant movement, 3
Ahluwalia, Montek S., 152
Ajitha Narayanan, 63
Alampalli forest, 111
Albania, 24
All India Coordination
    Committee of Communist
    Revolutionories, 17, 18, 19, 20,
    22
Amdal, Solveig, 128
Ananda Bazar Patrika, 50
Andhra Committee, 19
Andhra Prabha, 109
Andhra Pradesh, 37-46, 105
Andhra Pradesh Civil Liberties
    Committee, 147
Anjaiah, P., 116
Anti-Lin Biao, 94, 95, 101
Anti-Lin Biao faction, 114, 121, 126
Appalasuri, M., 40, 41, 97, 129
Assam, 64
Assault on images, 73
Atahualpa, Inca King, 150
Attacks on Police, 73-74

Baba Gurmukh Singh, 63
Baghaura - Dalelchack, 123
Bahujan Samaj Party, 128

Bangla Desh, 3, 87, 88, 89, 90
Banita Punji, 154
Basant Singh, 62
Basu, Jyoti, 51, 99
Battle of annihilation, 82
Bhagchashis, 6
Bhandari, Madan, 128
Bharadwaj, Krishna, 152
Bhaskar Rao, 45
Bhaskar Rao Malik, Nimmaluri,
    147
Bhavanapuram, 44
Bhojpur district, 95
Bholla, 62
Bhumi Sena, 125
Bihar, 54-58, 120-130
Bijli Singh, 54, 55
Birbhum, 47-53
Birsa Munda, 146
Bolpur, 52
Bose, Souren, 83, 99, 100, 170-171

Chandra Pulla Reddy, 45
Chandrapur, 118
Charan Singh, 98, 99
Charuism, 97
Chatterjee, Ashim, 48, 50, 62, 91,
    99, 100, 171
Chatterjee, Kanai, 121, 122
Chatterjee, Kshitish, 51
Che Guevara, 27, 148
Che Guevarism, 23
Chenna Reddy, 113
Chinese aggression, 6

195

Chinese Communist Party, 16, 19, 23, 83
Chota Nagpur, 56
Chou En-Lai, 88
Class enemies, 25, 26
Communist Bolshevik Party, 101
Communist Organisation of India (COI), 140
Communist Party of Ceylon, 20
Communist Party of Great Britain (ML), 23
Communist Party of India, 6, 8
Communist Party of Soviet Union, 16
Communist Unity Committee (M.L), 98
CPI(M) 15, 16, 17, 21, 40, 47, 100
CPI(ML), 21, 22, 23, 24, 26, 30, 32, 40, 45, 46, 52, 59, 60, 62, 65, 71, 76, 77, 82, 83, 87, 88, 89, 90, 98, 99, 100, 101, 106, 114, 121, 125, 126-129, 130, 140, 141, 180
Anti-Lin Biao faction, 145
First Party Congress, 30
CPI(ML) Liberation, 142
CP Reddy group, 114, 145
Cultural revolution, 70

Daggu Rayalingu, 109
Daggupati Chenchuramaiah, 110
Dakshin Desh, 121
Dalits, 158
Darjeeling, 8, 15
Das, Arvind S., 120, 147
Dasgupta, Biplab, 92, 144
Dasgupta, Pannalal, 11
Dasgupta, Parimal, 22, 53
Datta, Saroj, 171-172

Debro-Gopivallavpur, 33, 47, 48, 49, 50
Delhi, 64
Deng Xiao-ping, 144
Desai, Morarji, 98, 99
Digvijay Singh, 118
Dilip Banerjee group, 141
Donthe Markandeya, 115
Doragadda, 111

East Pakistan, 3, 87, 88
East Pakistan Communist Party (M.L), 89

Farzand Ahmad, 125

Gadchiroli, 118, 119
Gaddar, 112
Gandhi, Mahatma see Mahatma Gandhi
Gandhi, Rajiv, 154
Gangapur, 54, 55
Ganjam, 61
Gappu Guric, 39
Gaya district, 124
Ghosh, Biren, 51
Ghosh, Suniti Kumar, 23, 91, 97, 98, 105, 172
Ghosh Jayati, 152
Girijans, 38, 39, 40, 105, 146
Girijan insurgency, 37, 41, 42
Gopalan, K.P.R., 64
Gram Rakshak Dal, 55
Guerilla struggle, 26
Gunda boyina Anjaiah, 115
Gunupur Conspiracy Case, 61
Gupta, C.B., 59
Gupta, Ranjit, 74
Gurubux Singh, 91

Guzman, 150

Hoxha, Enver, 24
Hyderabad, 4

Indian Communist movement 3,
    12
Indian Communist Party, 165
Indian People's Front, 127, 142, 145

Jagadish Mahto, 96, 97
Jain, L.R., 153
Jain, Sumitra, 123
Jamshedpur, 57
Jamukula Katha, 39
Jana Adalat, 125
Janakiya Samskarika Vedi, 143
Jangal Mahal area, 121
Jangal Santhal, 6, 7, 9, 10, 91, 99,
    100, 174-175
Jan Natya Mandali, 112, 143, 147
Jawahar Rozgar Yojana, 154
Jayalalitha, 134
Jotedars, 6

K. Ramachandran faction, 140
Kaimur Range, 140
Kanai Kuity, 49
Kanshi Ram, 128
Karimnagar district, 112
Kedar Singh, 123
Kerala, 63
Kerala Communist Party, 140
Kharibari, 3, 5, 6, 9
Kisan Sabha, 4, 6
Kisan Sangram Samiti, 55
Konar, Hare Krishna, 9
Kondapalli Seetharamaiah, 105,
    106, 107, 108, 115

Koraput, 61
Krantikari Kisan Committee, 122
Krantikari Kisan Mazdoor Party,
    62
Krishna Kant, 99
Kuer Sena, 125
Kundan Ram, 61
Kunnikal Narayanan, 19, 64, 91

Lakeer, 62
Lakhimpur, 58
Lal Jhanda, 141
Lal Raksha Dal, 122, 125
Lal Sena, 125
Lapa Kishan, 3
Laqueur, Walter, 161
Latin America, 148
Laxmana Rao Ganapathy, M., 115
Liberation, 17, 27, 59, 77, 90
Liberation group, 126, 128, 140
Lin Biao, 22, 83, 94
Lokeswar Rao, C., 106
Lorik Sena, 125
LTTE, 114, 119, 134

Madhya Pradesh, 116-118
Magurjan village, 76
Maharashtra, 118-119
Mahatma Gandhi, 72
—— Statue, 58
Mahendragiri hills, 38
Mahendra Singh, 60, 91
Mahila Sravanthi, 108
Mandal Praja Parishad, 110
Maoist Communist Centre
    (MCC), 101, 121-126, 140, 143
Mao Tse-tung, 3, 17, 20, 21, 27, 29,
    30, 70, 144
—— thoughts, 11, 12

Mass Line, 60
Mayurbhanj, 61
Mazdoor Kisan Mukti Manch, 130
Mazdoor Kisan Sangathan, 108
Mazdoor Kisan Sangram Samiti,
  125, 129
Mazumdar Charu, 7, 17, 18, 20, 25,
  27, 28, 29, 32, 33, 37, 40, 41, 46,
  51, 61, 69, 70, 71, 72-76, 77,
  82-86, 90, 91, 92, 94, 95, 97, 105,
  108, 126, 135, 139, 142, 149,
  172-173, 178
Mazumdar, Khokan, 98
Midnapur, 47-53
Miller, Judith, 73
Mishra, Pramod, 122
Mishra, Shiv Kumar, 60, 83, 90
Mishra, Vinod, 126, 127, 142
Mishra, Jagannath, 61
Mitra, Jagannath, 61
Mitra, Subodh, 140
Mondal, Bhabadeb, 47, 48, 50
MMG group, 56, 57
Mujibur Rahman, 89
Mukherji, Ashutosh, 72
Mukherjee, Kalyan, 96
Mukherjee, Mahadeb, 95
Mukti Path, 60
Mukti Yudha, 88
Murmu, Gunadhar, 47, 48, 49, 50
Mushahari, 33, 54, 56
Myrdal, Gunnar, 6

Nagabhushanam Patnaik, 61, 83,
  91, 105, 127, 128
Naga Federal Government, 23
Nagi Reddy, 19, 45, 90
Nagi Reddy group, 97
Nanda, Jaladhar, 61

Narsinghpur, 55
New Age, 90
Natak Kala Kendra, 143
Naxalbari, 3-12, 25, 37, 139
Naxalbari of Bhojpur, 96
Naxalbari peasant struggle, 19, 180
Naxalbari uprising, 15, 16, 84
Naxalite groups, 114, 145
Naxalite guerillas, 55
Naxalite ideology, 160
Naxalite movement, 25, 29, 47, 92,
  139, 151, 156
Naxalite violence, 69, 131, 133
Nehru, Jawaharlal, 72
Nepal, 3
New Left, 101, 120-121
Nirmala Krishnamurthy, 45
Nishant Natya Manch, 143
Nizam, 4

Open Letter, 178-181
Operation Barga, 155
Operation Steeplechase, 81, 91
Orissa, 61, 87

Palia, 33, 58, 59
Panchadi Krishnamurthi, 39, 40
Panchadi Nirmala, 43
Paris Commune, 11
Parvathipuram Agency, 41, 42, 46
Pathak, Bindeshwar, 123
Patnaik, D.B.M., 61
Paul, Shanti, 141
Pawar, Sharad, 118
Peking, 3, 8, 15
People's court, 43, 113
People's Daily, 8, 23, 144
——, editorial, 165-169

People's Democratic Revolution, 18

People's Liberation Army, 46, 75-77, 135

People's Path, 62

People's War Group (PWG), 46, 101, 105-119, 133, 134, 139, 140, 141, 146, 147

Perunchitranar, 134

Phanas Punji, 154

Phani Bagchi group, 140

Phansidar, 3, 5

Planning Commission, 155

Poverty in India, 153

Prasad, Pradhan H., 121

Pro-Lin Biao, 94, 95, 101

Puber Hawa group, 53

Punjab, 62

Punjab Naxalites, 62

Quevedo, Franscisco de, 162

Rabi Das, 61

Radial Students Union, 108

Radial Youh League, 108

Rajkishor Singh, 91

Ramachandran, C.P., 145

Ramadhar Singh, 122

Ramamohan Rao, 114

Rama Rao, N.T., 110, 113

Rameshwar Ahir, 96, 97

Rampurhat, 52

Rana, Mihir, 49

Rana, Santosh, 47, 48, 49, 50, 62, 100, 173-174

Ranchi district, 57

Ratia Kishan, 3

Ravi Shankar, 140

'Red Area', 37, 43

Red Flag, 140

Red Gaurd Squads, 71

Red terror, 28

Revolutionary Communist group, 89

Revolutionary Writers, Association, 147

Roy, Apurba, 98

Roy, Jogu, 62

Roy, Rammohan, 73

Roy, Subroto, 57

Roychowdhary, Nagen, 9, 10

Roychowdhary, Sushital, 40, 73, 83, 90, 174

Roychowdhary, Bhowani, 129

Rupuskundi, 76

Ryotanga Sangram Samiti, 42

Rythu Coolie Sangham, 108

Sahajanand Saraswati, 146

Sahu, Ramesh Chandra, 45

Sainath, P., 14

Samal, Dinabandhu, 61

Sangu Kishan, 3

Sanjay Dusadh, 122

Sankaran Kutty Menon, A., 63

Sanmugathasan, 20, 24

Santhal Pargana, 5

Santosh Rana group, 114, 145

—— see also under Rana, Santosh

Sanyal, Kanu, 3, 7, 9, 10, 11, 12, 22, 40, 83, 91, 99, 100, 101, 122, 140, 143, 175

Saraf, Ram Piara, 63

Saraf group, 63

Sathyamurthy, K.G., 105, 108

Sathyanarayan Reddy, B., 108

Rupa/335/19-7-01

Satyanarayan Singh, 55, 69, 83, 84, 85, 86, 90, 97, 98, 99, 101, 176-177
Satyanarayan Singh, group, 98
Savarna Liberaton Front, 124
Scheduled Caste, 155, 156, 159
Scheduled Tribes, 155, 156, 159
Sen, Amulya, 121
Sen, Asit, 23, 175-176
Sen, Mary (*nee* Tyler), 176
    see also under Tyler
Sen, Sabuj, 140
Sen, Samar, 10
Senapati, Nagen, 49
Sethi group, 63
Shahid Minar Maidan, 100, 141
Shashtri, Lal Bahadur, 73
Shining Path Violence, 150
Siliguri, 9
Siliguri militants, 7
Singh, S.N., *see* Satyanarayan Singh
Singhbhum, 57
Sivenji, 122
Sohal, J.S., 63
Spring Thunder, 180
S.R. Bhaiji group, 145
Srikakulam, 33, 37-46, 151
Srikakulam martyrs, 51
Srikakulam struggle, 19
Srinivas Reddy, K., 113
Subbarao Panigrahi, 39, 45
Sundaram, K. 153
Suri, 52

Tagore, Rabindranath, 72, 73
Talukdar, Subir, 141
Tamil Nadu Liberation Front, 134
Tamil Nadu Viduthalali Padai, 134

Tebhaga movement, 4
Tajeswara Rao, C., 39, 40, 41, 83
Telengana, 106, 109, 151
Telengana insurrection, 4
Telengana struggle, 105
Telugu Desam, 110
Tendulkar, S.D., 153
Tewari, Vishwanath, 59
Thamada Ganapathy, 41, 45
Thamizharasan, 134
Tyler, Mary, 56

Umadhar Singh, 140
United Nations Development Programme, 154, 157, 158
Uttar Pradesh, 58-60

Vairagi, Baburam, 63
Vasquez, Fabio, 149
Vempatapu Satyanarayana, 39, 40, 41, 44, 46
Venkateswara Rao, Potturi, 109
Venu, K., 134
Vidyasagar, Iswar Chandra, 72
Vinyan, Dr., 129
Vitthal Rao, Gummadi, 112

Wangdi, Sonam, 9
Wangdi, T., 6
Warsaw Pact, 19
West Bengal, 47-53
West Bengal State Kisan Conference, 6

Yadav, Rajendra Singh, 96
Yahya Khan, 87, 88, 90
Yatindra Kumar group, 140
Yugantuk, 65